First published 2018

Studies on the Development Characteristics of the Innovation System in the Major Countries of ASEAN: Focus on Vietnam, Indonesia, Myanmar, and Laos

Byeouk-Gyu Lee

Dae-Woo Cho

Myung-Bae Yeom

Gi-Don An

15, Olympic-ro 78-gil, Gangdong-gu, Seoul, Republic of Korea

TEL +82-2-309-5356

ISBN 979-11-86331-46-0

Price: 30.00$

Printed in Korea

This work was supported by the Ministry of Education of the Republic of Korea and the National Research Foundation of Korea(NRF-2015S1A3A2046546)

Contents

Chapter 3 Innovation System in Vietnam

Chapter 4 Innovation System in Indonesia

Chapter 5 Innovation System in Myanmar

Chapter 1 Introduction

The purpose of this research is to compare developmental characteristics of the innovation system in the major countries of ASEAN, which are on the transformation. This research assumes that the type of economic system has a major impact on the development of the innovation system. In addition, the economic system in the major countries of ASEAN are on the transformation. There is therefore a need for research to include transformation as an important factor in the development of the innovation system.

Scientific contributions that deal with the development of civic engagement, especially transformation, in democratization contexts exist above all with the "new democracies" that emerged after the collapse of the Soviet Union in Eastern and Southeastern Europe. Few works have concrete examples of democratization in Asia as a research topic; Innovation systems in democratic transitions in Asia are considered to be even rarer. The research contributions to the relations between transformation and innovation systems in Southeast Asia are limited to individual case studies of social movements. So far, a macro-perspective study on the "innovation system in the context of transformation trends" has been missing, making this work an important contribution to research whose relevance extends beyond the cases in Southeast Asia.

What is an innovation system, how can you explain it? Which elements does an innovation system possess? What is the "national or regional" of an innovation system? The next chapter is about it.

In this study, education is considered an important element of the innovation system. Education is a key sector for sustainable social and economic development, laying the groundwork for the country's ability to fight poverty and achieve the Millennium Development Goals (MDGs). Education is also a core element of the innovation system. Education is also an important factor in raising environmental awareness and the sustainable use of natural resources indispensable to economic and social development in Southeast Asia.

This study also assumes that the economic and social system surrounding the innovation system has a strong impact on the innovation system. That is, there is a relationship between the innovation system and the types of economy.

In the methodological aspect, this study is also understood as a descriptive theory that uses a conceptual framework to describe how things develop and change. Conceptual frameworks and analysis heuristics that do not specify causal relationships between concepts are not considered as explanatory theory, but rather as descriptive theory. Descriptive theory aims to improve categorization schemes to better identify the relevant attributes of a phenomenon. The theory of explanation formulates assumptions with theoretical terms (often based on categorization schemes) about relationships and conditions to which they apply. Explanations can be given at various levels of abstraction with theoretical or observable concepts. Methodically, this presents itself as a descriptive theory.

Chapter 2 Theoretical Background

I. Innovation System

1. National innovation system

Friedrich List is considered the "father" of the National Innovation System: economists and politicians (1789-1846). His concept is "national production systems" [1]: optimization of production, national infrastructure and institutions. Christopher Freeman formulated the term "National System of Innovation" (1982) and further developed List's idea.

„…the elements and relationships which interact in the production, diffusion and use of new, and economically useful knowledge (…) and are either located within or routed inside the borders of a nation state. “ (Lundvall 1992)

In this sense, Freeman considers it necessary for the state to promote the technological infrastructure and to make it clear that short-term strategies (such as wage and currency changes) have only limited effectiveness in strengthening the international competitiveness of an economy.[2]

---

1) List, F., The National System of Political Economy, Kindle Edition 2008

Bengt-Ake Lundvall is regarded as the founder of the NIS concept.[3)] According to his point of view, innovation is more inherent part of the normal economic activities. Interactive learning is at the core of his approach.

Fig. 1: Model of the research and innovation system

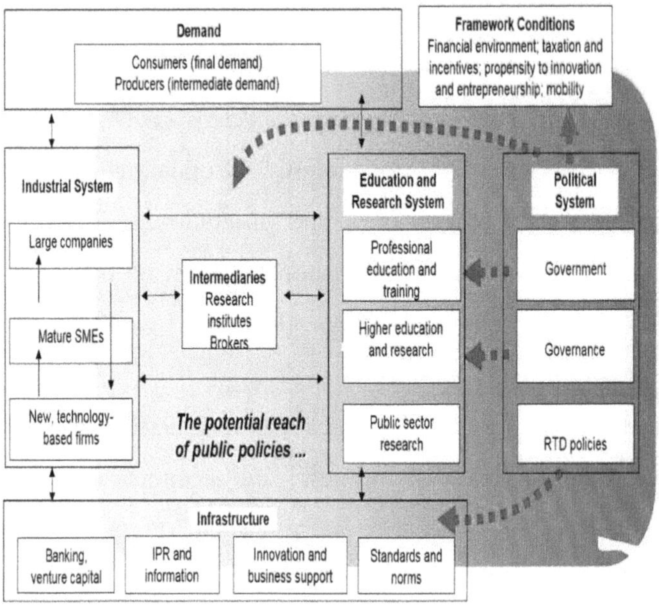

Source: Technopolis 2000, modified and extended by S. Kuhlmann, Fraunhofer ISI, https://www. isi-lehre.de/lehre-wAssets/docs/hannover/ vergleich_innosystem /folien/Innovationssystem.pdf

2) Freeman, C. The 'National System of Innovation' in historical perspective, Cambridge Journal of Economics, Volume 19, Issue 1, 1 February 1995, Pages 5-24

3) Lundvall, B-A., National Systems of Innovation. Towards a Theory of Innovation and Interactive Learning, Pinter Publishers, London. 1992

There is no generalized definition of a National Innovation System. What is important is the network of interaction or system. The concept of National Innovation System is based on the premise that understanding links between innovators is crucial to improving technology performance. Innovation and technological advancement are the result of a complex set of relationships between actors that produce, distribute and apply different types of knowledge.[4)]

The following points can be presented as elements of a National Innovation System, as shown in Fig. 1.[5)]

(1) Institutional structures of a country: They are formed by companies, universities, research and training institutions, standards, routines, networks, financial institutions, and government measures to promote and regulate technological change.

(2) Incentive system of a country: This includes among others incentive systems for innovation, for technology transfer, for learning and qualification, for start-ups and occupational mobility in and between organizations.

(3) Skills and creativity of the innovation and economic actors of a country: Both between countries and between companies in a country, there are huge differences in the diversity

---

4) Marinova, R., & Phillimore, J., Models of innovation. In V. Shavinina(Ed.), International handbook on innovation. Amsterdam: Elserver, 2003.

5) Fraunhofer Institut System- und Innovationsforschung, https://www.isi-lehre.de/lehre-wAssets/docs/hann over/vergleich_innosystem/folien/Innovationssystem.pdf

and quality of products and services, as well as the opportunities to develop new development paths.

(4) Cultural peculiarities of a country: The cultural features are also reflected, for example, in different acceptance and understanding of usage of technology.

To improve the lack of functional integration in the linear models, the fourth generation innovation process model (the interactive approach) was developed. This is also known as the integrated business process model. The ever-shortening product life cycle, has led to the improved cooperation between research, development and production and also improved horizontal cooperation, regardless of company boundaries. Therefore, it is also considered to pursue a time-based strateg y.[6] This approach views the innovation process as parallel activities across organizational functions. Therefore, Combinations of push and pull models, integration within a firm, emphasis the importance of external linkages.

2. Regional innovation system

Regional innovation systems (RIS or RSI) are referred to as "geographical distinctive, interlinked organizations supporting innovation and those conducting it, mainly firms" (Cooke et al.,

---

6) Rothwell R., "Towards the fifth-generation innovation process" in International Marketing Review. 11(7): 7-31, 1994.

1996). The Regional Innovation System can theoretically be linked to the network model of the innovation process, such as the National Innovation System. The network of internal and external stakeholders and the connections between all role players are important in this model.[7]

While earlier studies focused on regional support systems (with a strong reference to regional innovation policy),[8] today it is a knowledge application subsystem (regional companies and their customers, suppliers, competitors and cooperation partners) and the knowledge production and diffusion subsystem (universities and other research institutions, transfer organizations, training institutes).[9] It is precisely this differentiation that has shifted the focus of analysis within the institutional framework to the relationship between scientific institutions and companies and the mediating role of the state.

---

7) Cooke, P., Uranga, M.G., Etxebarria, G., Regional innovation systems: Institutional and organisational dimensions, Research Policy Volume 26, Issues 4-5, December 1997, Pages 475-491

8) Cooke, P., Uranga, M.G., Etxebarria, G., Regional Systems of Innovation: An Evolutionary Perspective, Environment and Planning A, volume 30, pages 1563 - 1584, 1998.

9) Fornahl, D., & Brenner, T., Cooperation, Networks and Institutions in Regional Innovation Systems, Edward Elgar Publishing Ltd, 2003.

Fig. 2: Regional Innovation System

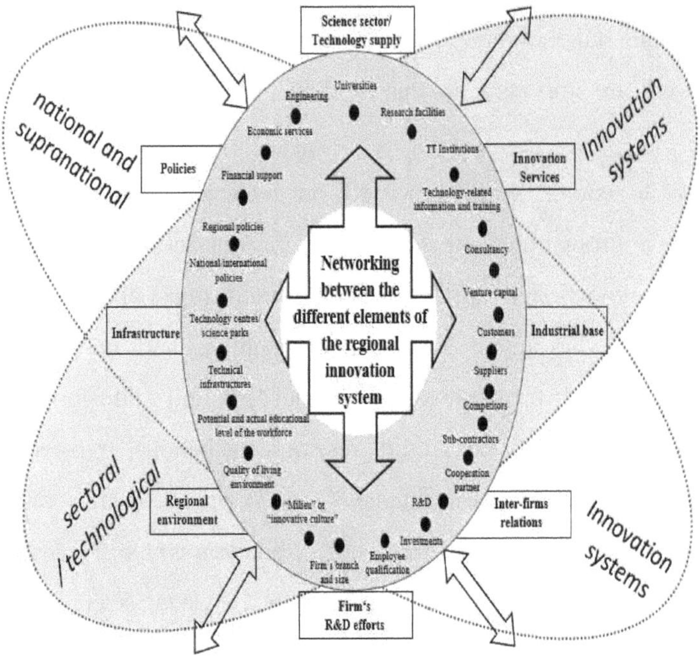

Source: Design by K. Koschatzky, Fraunhofer ISI, https://www.isi-lehre.de/lehre-wAssets/docs/hannover/vergleich_innosystem /folien/Innovationssystem.pdf

In the available definitions of innovation systems, the concept of the institution plays a dominant role. Stakeholders or role-players can be called institutions here. In other words, innovation systems are usually defined institutionally. In all the definitions used, various economic, social and political institutions that influence innovation are central elements and are not taken away. Examples of such institutions are universities, R&D laboratories, schools, patent systems, labor market organizations, banking systems, various government agencies, etc. There are also other types of institutions in the sense of norms, habits, practices and routines that have very important influences on innovation and innovation systems.[10)]

Both of National Innovation System (NIS) and Regional Innovation System (RIS) can be linked to the Network Model of the innovation process, however, norms, habits, practices and routines are not given any value in the literatures on National Innovation System, while they are emphasized in the context of embedding regional innovation activities in the literatures on the Regional Innovation System. The core of the Regional Innovation System discussion is that interactive learning based on tacit knowledge, geographical proximity, and common value shared geographically are key to the process of innovation. The space here does not mean physical space, rather, it is close to a cultural space in terms of the sharing of the value system. In this regard, Regional Innovation System can be classified as Innovation System 3.0.[11)]

---

10) Marinova, R., & Phillimore, J., Models of innovation. In V. Shavinina(Ed.), International handbook on innovation. Amsterdam: Elserver, 2003.

11) Trippl, M., Maier, G., Tödtling, F., Regional- und Stadtökonomik 2: Regional Entwicklung und Regional Politik, Wiesbaden, 2012 (Trippl, M., Maier, G., Tödtling, F., Regional and Urban Economics 2: Regional Development and Regional Policy, Wiesbaden, 2012)

Major characteristics of the network model are the influence of external environment and the effective communication with the external environment. Innovation happens within a network of internal and external stakeholders. It is important therefore is to establish links between all the role-players (See Fig. 2). Collaboration with external research organizations and marketing is much stronger than in the fourth generation.[12)]

II. Economic System

Is there an economic system besides the social system or does the economic system belong to it? The discussion about the economic and social system has been conducted largely on the one hand as criticism of the existing and on the other hand as development of proposals for reforms. Although questions of the economic system were envisaged; However, a conceptual separation of the economic and social system did not develop until the emergence of economics or national economy and sociology as sciences. It is still controversial today.

On the other hand, in sociological and - in so far as they use the system-theoretical terminology - in economic studies, there is broad agreement on the definition of three to four large

---

12) Edquist, C. (ed.), Systems of Innovation, Technologies, Institutions and Organizations, Oxon, 2005.

subsystems. This division of society into a political, an economic, a social and a cultural system goes back to Parsons.

Schueller differs from the existing type of economic system: a) the Soviet-type central administrative economy, b) the socialist market economy of a state-socialist type, and c) the market economy as decentralized economic planning in several variants.[13] Moreover, former Soviet economic system, this book treats the free market economy and the social market economy as two variants of the market economy.

In the context of the free market economy alone, the market determines which products or services are offered in what quantity and at what price. Prerequisites for this economic form are, among other things, free competition, free choice of profession and free pricing. A special form is the social market economy, in which free competition. The opposite of the free market economy is the planned economy, in which only the state controls the supply. is restricted by laws and state intervention.

---

13) Schueller, A. (1990), Probleme des Uebergangs von der Staatswirtschaft zur Marktwirtschaft, in: Forschungsstelle(ed.); Problems of the transition from the state economy to the market economy, in: Research Center (ed.) 1-24.

1. Former soviet economic system

After the experiences of the world economic crisis of 1929 and post-war poverty after 1945, the planned economic model appeared to many, including social democrats and trade unionists in West Germany, as a promising alternative to the market economy with its uncontrolled forces. The advantages seemed to be obvious: a production according to the previously determined needs; optimal utilization of the means of production and no waste of resources due to overproduction; Concentration of economic power on priority projects and coordination of technical developments; overall, a well-planned management that would ensure crisis resistance and full employment. Critics, on the other hand, warned that a command economy with rigid targets was unable to respond flexibly to market signals; that any economic dynamism would be hindered by immense bureaucratic steering and steering effor t.[14)]

The structure of the classical socialist system can be represented by five constituent elements that form a causality line:[15)]

(1) Sovereign power of the Communist Party, primacy of official ideology

(2) Dominant position of state property

---

14) Pasler, S. Die sozialistische Planwirtschaft der DD. Konrad-Adenauer-Stiftung e.V., Sankt Augustin/Berlin[The socialist planned economy of the GDR]

15) Kornai, Janos: The Socialist System, Oxford, 1992

(3) Supremacy of bureaucratic coordination

(4) Plan economy, soft budget barriers, paternalistic behavior of superiors, weak price sensitivity

(5) Forced growth, chronic shortage, labor shortages and unemployment at work.

The classical system is viable for some time under the described causalities, but is increasingly burdened by economic problems, public dissatisfaction, loss of the self-confidence of the rulers, and so on. Over time, the problems and contradictions of the classical system became clear and led to its changes.[16)]

The socialist system has changed constantly over time to eliminate the malfunctioning that has occurred since the 1950s. The changes were different in the individual socialist countries and came in two forms: improvements and reforms. Perfection does not change the constituent elements of the socialist system, such as the reorganization of ministries that split or merge. By reforms of the socialist system we mean changes in the individual elements of a socialist economic system, or change in the constituent features of the system, without taking the system out of the family of socialist systems. Although reforms have led to systemic changes, e.g. greater liberalization and decentralization of the economy, but the power of the

16) Kornai, Janos, ibid.

communist parties, as the most important constitutive feature of the socialist system, remained untouched. A turnaround within the system is nevertheless accomplished.[17)]

2. Free market economy

At the end of the 18th century, economists founded the market economy. They described it as a system that transforms individual egoism into social benefit. The principle of the market with its regulation by supply and demand was recognized. In the classical model of the market economy, one achieves the highest prosperity for society by practicing economic behavior through selfishness (self-directed behavior) and complete competition.

The free market economy is an economic form in which only the market (supply and demand) determines which products and services are produced and offered in which quantity and at what price.

The conditions for a free market economy include free competition, free choice of profession and free pricing. In addition, the means of production must be privately owned and economic factors such as land and labor freely accessible.

The classical theory of the market economy is closely linked to the social theory of liberalism (liberalism is a way of think-

17) Kornai, Janos, ibid.

ing and a way of life that stands for autonomy, responsibility and free development of the personality).

In 1940, Walter Eucken worked out the market economy (and also the central administration economy as the counterpart) to basic forms of economic systems.

An essential feature of the market economy is the private ownership of means of production. Entrepreneurs who possess means of production or rights of disposal are also called "capitalists". They decide on the way of production. The sections are governed by the market, which represents the confluence of supply and demand.

The market economy is an economic order. Often it is also referred to by other terms:

- Free economy
- competitive economy
- transport economics
- capitalism or money economy

Their essential features are:

- the existence of a market and competition among each other,
- private property and
- a money-driven economy.

Market economy is an economic order in which production and consumption are determined by the price freely generated in the market. Individual economic agents decide on service provision and consumption. The markets are the coordinating centers on which supply and demand are coordinated. This form of market economy is the ideal of liberalism. In this free market economy, state intervention becomes superfluous when balancing the interests and automatically resulting maximum goods supply. However, restricting competition through cartels and the formation of monopolies has led to crises and an anti-social distribution of power.

In the case of a fundamental affirmation of the system, the demand for state intervention became ever stronger. The social market economy was developed. A. Mueller-Armack coined the designation for the aimed particularly in the Federal Republic of Germany economic order. Political enforcement experienced this form of market economy by the Minister of Economics Ludwig Erhard.

3. Social market economy

The German economic system is called social market economy. Free competition is limited by law and government intervention to ensure social security and social progress. An example of this state intervention is the social insurance obligation.

Social market economy affirms the right to private property, personal responsibility of the entrepreneur and willingness to take risks as a basic requirement of free market economy. At the same time, these basic requirements are linked to a system of social protection. This protection is expressed in the institutional safeguarding of competition (prevention of the abuse of power by cartels and monopolies), securing the fullest possible employment and monetary stability and social income redistribution.

At the end of the Second World War, the model of the social market economy was born. Their spiritual fathers, Walter Eucken and A. Mueller-Armack, united therein the ideas of neoliberalism and the Christian social doctrine. The Federal Minister of Economics and later Federal Chancellor Ludwig Erhard(1897-1977) politically enforced this economic order in the Federal Republic of Germany.

The term "social" stands for social justice and security, "market economy" includes the individual and economic freedom as well as the market and decentralized coordination of economic activities. Within this economic order, the state has the task of preventing or mitigating undesirable effects of the market economy. He should restrict the individual liberties where they jeopardize social justice and security. The state takes z. This includes, for example, the distribution of income and wealth (support for the sick, the disabled and the socially disadvantaged), since market distribution only takes into account those who actively participate in the economic process.

The basic idea of economic freedom is expressed in many ways in the social market economy:

- demands can freely decide which goods and services they consume (freedom from consumption);
- owners of means of production have free choice as to whether and to whom they provide their mental and physical labor, material assets and entrepreneurial skills (freedom of trade, freedom of occupation, freedom of use of property and property rights);
- producers have the freedom to decide which goods and services they produce to the extent and on the market (freedom of production).

Consumers and entrepreneurs are subject to freedom of competition. In competition, business entities aim for a specific goal. The higher degree of target achievement of one usually results in a lower degree of target achievement of the other. Free competition ensures coordination of the economic activities of consumers and producers. This leads to a price formation on the market. The prices show the suppliers in which areas their production factors are used most favorably and the customers have the opportunity to judge how they can best satisfy their needs.

In order for free competition to ensure a good market supply, it must fulfill several functions (competition functions):

- Governance function - providing businesses with an offer of goods and services that meets consumer needs;
- Allocation function - Use of production processes that ensure the greatest possible factor utilization efficiency;
- Innovation function - promoting and realizing technical and scientific progress to enable new and cheaper products and production processes;
- Adaptation function - flexible adaptation of production to constantly changing economic data;
- Distribution function - ensuring a fair income distribution;
- Control function - control and limitation of economic power.

The enforcement of the competitive system of the social market economy requires a proper competitive order. There are several reasons for this:

- Competition is not self-evident in all markets, but is tied to the creation of structural and institutional conditions.
- Competition must be limited in content, as not every form of behavior and form of competition leads to economically efficient results.
- The competition must be protected. On the one hand, on economic agents who are inclined to avoid competitive pressure but who want to be involved in overall economic success (freeloaders) and, on the other hand, of micro-economic interests that aim to falsify or restrict competition.

The fight against unfair competition and the safeguarding of free competition against restrictions are among the important tasks of the competitive order. In order to fulfill these two laws were passed.

- Law against Restraints of Competition (GWB)

The UWG is supplemented by the Act against Restraints of 1958 (now six amendments). It is intended to protect the freedom of competition from a point of view of economic policy against a "legacy" of the markets. The GWB meets important regulations on antitrust law, the abuse control of dominant companies and the concentration control of companies.

- Disadvantaged companies and regions

However, there are also companies, sectors of activity (eg agriculture and mining) and economic regions that are at a competitive disadvantage or are no longer competitive. Here the state can grant subsidies (subsidies).

Aid is, directly or indirectly, state transfer payments that directly or indirectly favor beneficiaries without adequate consideration in accordance with selected criteria, and which result in direct costs or revenue shortfalls for public budgets. The aid is in most cases aimed at promoting or alleviating economic difficulties. At first glance, such support is perceived positively by the beneficiaries. In reality, this will only postpone the necessary restructuring measures. Non-promoted competitors rate state aid as discrimination and feel disadvantaged in the competitive environment.

III. Decentralization and Governance

1. Decentralization

Governmental and administrative systems are accompanied by a redistribution of influence, power positions and resources and influence the territorial distribution of power by changing interstate intergovernmental relations.[18)]

Although analyzes of institutional reforms in transition contexts and young democracies have increased in numbers, research in this area is still in its infancy. Roughly speaking, two directions of investigation can be distinguished, which are closely related empirically and theoretically and stimulate each other. One addresses the impact of institutions and material policies or external actors on democratization and / or consolidation. This is the predominant research direction within neo-institutionalism. The focus of the other perspective is on

18) Baldersheim, Illner, Wollmann, Local Democracy in Post-Communist Europe, Springer, 2003

the development of institutions under the conditions of transition. There is still a need for research, especially for this perspective, although the wave of democratization that began in southern Europe and continued in Latin America, East Asia and Eastern Europe has stimulated preoccupation with institutions and their genesis as dependent variables in different contexts.[19)]

Especially the multiplicity and simultaneity of the reform processes in East Central Europe since 1989 not only empirically enlivened entire research branches within the social sciences, they were also an important incentive for the methodically conscious analysis. In addition to political and (whose organizational theory interested subdiscipline) administrative science, sociology, political geography and economics in particular have dealt with the decentralization phenomenon in post-socialist states. Systematically comparative and theoretically demanding investigations are, of course, the exception. More frequently, the work is more descriptive or balancing. The research gap is even greater when it comes to inter-regional comparative analyzes that abstract from the supposed post-socialist exceptionality.[20)]

19) Stöver, Philip, Demokratisierung und Dezentralisierung, Staatsorganisationsreformen im Kontext von Regime- und Regierungswechseln in Spanien, Polen und Großbritannien, 2012

20) Baldersheim, Illner, Wollmann, Local Democracy in Post-Communist Europe, Springer, 2003

2. Governance

The discussions about governance have given new impetus to political science debates: the focus on political results is tentative, it seems at first glance, in the background and the political process is gaining in relevance. New terms such as 'strong democracy' (Barber 1994), 'deliberative democracy' (Habermas 1996) and 'participatory governance' (Grote and Gbikpi 2002) have conquered the debate and point to participatory forms, either local decentralized activities or direct democratic elements or network-based collaborations are more important. More transparency and co-determination stand for more democracy; As a result, the demands for a more transparent and participatory policy, at least at a generally binding level, are formulated in most governance analyzes.[21)]

The concept of governance combines - as most studies have emphasized - with changes in the political-administrative system as well as the consequences of globalization and deregulation (Benz 2004). The concept of governance points to new forms of cooperation in which the state no longer mediates between the different interests as a controlling center but as a so-called interdependence manager. The concept of governance implies, on the one hand, that participation in governing involves not

21) Einig, Klaus; Grabher, Gernot; Ibert, Oliver; Strubelt, Wendelin (Hgg.): Urban Governance, in: Informationen zur Raumentwicklung, Heft 9/10, 2005.

only an indirect participation in "government affairs" over elections, but also broader political engagement in public life. (Kleinfeld, Plamper et al. 2006).

Although occasionally democratic questions and arguments are taken up in the governance analyzes, in almost all investigations they remain strangely disconnected from the actual questions of implementation and problem-solving. The complexity of the Governance Arrangements just includes just a lot of disadvantages: eg. The opaqueness of the structures and processes for many outsiders, but also many participants, is enormous. As a result, responsibilities may be more concealed than disclosed, and at the same time the mergers may be a deterrent to many stakeholders. Governance analysis rarely addresses this problem, which is why Peters and Pierre (2003) interpret the investigations as a naive attempt to ignore conflicts and power relations and instead emphasize strategic dimensions of change through forms of governance, including: the re-legitimization and/or strengthening of trust against the citizens.

Jessop (2002) and Haus (2007) make a distinction between governance and metagovernance, which in the latter case focuses on the strategic activities of the state (including various activities such as the consideration of market, hierarchical and network relations). This differentiation or elaboration of the different strategies can be extremely informative for governance analysis. Sommerville argues in his article on "Governance and Democratic Transformation" that citizens (organized or dis-organized) can participate in a series of governance arrangements, but only within "overall regulatory or disciplinary" frameworks set by governments. (Sommerville 2004: 6)

Taking into account the aspects mentioned above, the following problem areas become relevant when dealing with the topics of governance and civic participation: Firstly, it deals with a changed prioritization of legitimacy and effectiveness as well as with power issues and dominance structures. Secondly, discussions at the individual level are relevant - the Thirdly, the development of self-competence and the ability to participate, thirdly, the negotiation modes and decision-making processes of the different forms of participation. Fourth, the processes of internal social change, for example the role of social networks, are relevant.

And finally, fifthly, ideological value discussions such as justice, sustainability and gender democracy, which are interwoven in a cross-sectional manner with the first four areas, play an important role. The sketching of the topics makes it clear that, although questions of political science are at the center, answering the questions also requires an interdisciplinary streak of sociological, environmental-psychological and environmental-scientific analyzes.

IV. Transformation

The literature often talks about transformation, but without to give a clear indication of whether it is a temporally and spatially separate process or a general transformation or transformation of the traditional political or economic system. In this sense, transformation becomes a complex and multi-layered transformation of social, political and economic

Shapes described. Since the previous theories of transformation derived from the neoliberal theorists focused on the transformation of the economic system "integration into the global division of labor". Or, according to Altvater[22], under the given world-historical circumstances, the transformation of the economic system means "integration into the global division of labor", and this transformation is largely determined by the logic and power of globalized capital. they had overlooked the conceptions of sociopolitical transformation, such as a fundamental social question and the transformation of the society social system. It has not been fully implemented within democratic institutions or in full compliance with democratic principles and practices. The following section deals with economic transformation and social transformation.

22) Altvater, E. (1998), p 7-12

1. Economic transformation

Depending on the author, there are different conceptual understandings about economic transformation, some of which are presented here.

Eucken starts from more concrete economic forms of the market, but extends his consideration of the transformation over the economic area to connections between social areas. It expresses the development or transformation of market forms from the demand monopoly to complete competition, the tendency for state intervention and centralized state steering, and the transition from private to collective ownership as transformation.[23)]

23) Eucken, W. (1952), Grundsätze der Wirtschaftspolitik. Bern, Tübingen; Principles of economic policy. Bern, Tübingen p. 46. Before the order theoretical work of Eucken, who conceived an ORDO idea in the 40's, there was social-economic work. An example is Bukharin. Under the old term "transformation", which Bukharin used in the socioeconomic sense, one understands the general theory of the transformation process as the process of transforming capitalist society into communist society. For this transformation the complete political and economic collapse of the old society is presupposed. Its term refers to the Marxist term "period of revolutionary transformation, transitional period and social transformation", and at the same time the idea the dominance of this or that area plays a role. According to Bukharin, the transformation is not confined to isolated features or realms, but is seen as an interdependence of different realms. Bucharin, N (1920, 1922, 1989) : Ökonomik der Transformationsperiode, Hamburg :Verlag der kommunistischen Internationale 1922, russ.: Ekonomila perechodnogo perioda. Moskava: GOSIZDAT, 1920, Nachdruck verschiedener Kapitel in : Bucharin, N.L. : Problemy teorii i praktiki sozializma.

The economic order subdivides Eucken into the free "transport economy" and "centrally-managed administrative economy". In the centrally-managed administration economy, he distinguishes one type from private property and one from collective ownership of means of production. His theoretical hypothesis is, as several authors have called the inter-dependence of the various areas, not a limited economic, but constitution, economic constitution and social order. He is also interested in the connection between the economic order and the social question.[24)]

The transport economy, which is coordinated by markets, as an alternative to the central administration economy, emphasizes the competitive order, in which the market form of complete competition dominates. These normative principles as ORDO idea assume that the different situations of the individual countries are to be considered. These constituent and regulatory principles can be consulted in different situations of transition countries.[25)]

This results in a number of conditions that must be met for the market economy, which are described below[26)] :

24) Eucken, W. (1952), ibid.

25) ibid.

26) Kloten, N. (1993), The Time Dimension of the Transition of Economic Systems. In: Wagener HJ. (eds) On the Theory and Policy of Systemic Change. Studies in Contemporary Economics. Physica-Verlag HD

- The granting of individual rights of action and property (or property rights) as the core of a private law regime
- Decentralization and unbundling of state-owned enterprises
- Forms of transfer of ownership from state hands to private hands
- A reorganization of the banking system with a strict separation between central bank and - competing - commercial banks
- A comprehensive restructuring of state budget management and the system of levies
- The abandonment of the hitherto customary systematic use of monetary funds to state funds in favor of self-reliant financial disposition of companies with simultaneous regular collection of taxes
- Adequate opening of markets to foreign markets on the basis of compliant exchange rates.

Under the economic conceptions, comprehensive definition is proposed today. A transformation of the economic order should be understood as any substitution of others - even individual - of order-constituting characteristics by which the old (partial) order is replaced by a new one. At the same time, the goal of a complete transformation towards the market economy should at least be recognizable.[27)]

In the transformation, in the sense of no transfer, but of a new creation, it is the total change of the constitutive order forms of the given economic system. As such, in the theory of order, the forms of planning of economic processes that determine the coordination mechanism of the economic system and the forms of ownership that particularly affect economic efficiency are considered. Decentralized forms of planning and market coordination of the individual plans, which combine with predominantly private ownership of the means of production, characterize the market-economy and capitalist economic systems. In comparison, central planning of the economic processes in connection with state ownership of the means of production are the constitutive forms of order in the central administrative economies or in the socialist economic system s.[28)]

Economic transformation presupposes that transformation theory is observed from the perspective of the economist.

In the twentieth century, neoclassical economics was used as the theoretical basis for economic models. In contrast to classical art, in which individual action is considered against the background of belonging to a class (method and central question arise from the integration of price and distribution theory

27) ibid, p. 26

28) Eucken, W. (1952), Grundsätze der Wirtschaftspolitik. Bern, Tübingen; Principles of economic policy. Bern, Tübingen

into a theory of social classes), neoclassical theory is above all the logical one Application of methodological individualism and the assumption of rationally acting individuals (homines oeconomici), who act on markets on the basis of subjective utility calculations, starting point of economic modeling.[29)]

Methodological individualism states that the description of economic processes is based on the actions of individuals. This term is to be distinguished from political individualism. This is based on general principles and makes a number of practical statements. The methodological individualism, however, claims nothing and has no special requirements.[30)]

Classical and neoclassical are by their very nature not suitable for describing the transformation process and are understood to be [...] the science of the behavior and action of human beings in relation to the solution of the allocation problem of resources and the distribution of production to the satisfaction of human beings Needs [...]. They place economic phenomena in a price-theoretical context and evaluate them according to the value theory. Both theories are less explanations of the economic systems in which they came into being, but rather their

---

29) Feess-D rr, Eberhard: Eine Einfuehrung in die klassische und klassisch-neoricardianische Preis und Verteilungstheorie, Marburg 1992. [An Introduction to Classical and Classical-Neoricardian Price and Distribution Theory, Marburg]

30) Henry, J. F.: The making of neoclassical economics, Boston 1990.

outcome and legitimacy. They thus exclude the explanation of the transformation process.[31)]

With institutional economics, neoclassicism continued to develop. Traditional institutional economics emerged from the neglect of the role of institutions by classical and neoclassical theory and emphasized the need to consider institutional structures in explaining economic processes. The resulting theoretical models are used to partially analyze political, economic, and sociocultural phenomena of micro-level transformation. Although with the help of the institutions economics[32)] interdisciplinary theorizing like e.g. the property rights and public choice theory: it has not been able to produce a comprehensive, interdisciplinary modeling at the macro level, which could theoretically explain the transformation process in its entirety. This requires the development of interdisciplinary models and interdisciplinary approaches far beyond the perspective of the economist.[33)]

---

31) Henry, J. F. ibid.

32) For an economic systematization of the concept of institution cf. Wellesen, Iris (1994), Zur Auslegung des Institutionenbegriffs in der Soziologie [On the interpretation of the concept of institution in sociology]

33) Vanberg, Viktor: Der individualistische Ansatz zu einer Theorie der Entstehung und Entwicklung von Institutionen, in: Jahrbuch für Neue Politische Ökonomie, hrsg. von Erik Boettcher, Philipp Herder-Dorneich und Karl-Ernst Schenk, Bd. 2, Tübingen 1983, [The Individualistic Approach to a Theory of the Origin and Development of Institutions, in: Jahrbuch für Neue Politische Ökonomie, ed. by Erik Boettcher, Philipp Herder-Dorneich and Karl-Ernst Schenk, vol. 2] p. 50-69.

2. Social transformation

Transformation is a process of simultaneous change of the entire social system, the economic, political, legal and behavioral levels as social subsystems. There is a difference between economics and political science in terms of the concept of transformation: in economics, it is assumed that economic liberalization and growth precede democratization. Political theories, on the other hand, presuppose the integrity of the state, democratic rules and the elimination of the social, ethnic and religious divisions of democratization and the realization of functioning markets. Essentially, it's about building institutions.[34)]

Among other things, this includes the creation of new structures, rules, approval procedures and behavioral norms that influence people's behavior. The transformation as the transformation of the whole social System can only be terminated when all transformation levels have changed, in fact:[35)]

---

34) Boxberger, Gerald: Sozialpolitik und Transformationsprozesse: Kosten der polnischen Transformation und ihre Minderung ueber staatliche Sozialpolitik und Selbsthilfeinitiativen, Frankfurt am Main, 1997, p. 17. [Social Policy and Transformation Processes: Cost of Polish Transformation and its Reduction on State Social Policy and Self-Help Initiatives.]

35) Wolf, Michael: Transformation als Systemwechsel eine modelltheoretische Annäherung. In: Hopfmann, Arndt; Wolf, Michael (Hrsg.): Transformation und Interdependenz. Beiträge zu Theorie und Empirie der mittel- und osteuropäischen Systemwechsel (Politische Soziologie, Band 12), Münster, 1998, [Transformation as a system change ?? a model-theoretical approach. In: Hopfmann, Arndt; Wolf, Michael (ed.): Transformation and Interdependence. Contributions to theory and empiricism of the medium and Eastern European System Change (Politische Soziologie, Vol. 12)], Münster, 1998 p. 59.

- Economic level: from the planned economy to the democratic market economy
- Political level: from dictatorship to democracy
- Behavioral level: from dogmatism to relativism
- Legal level: From a party ideological legal system to civil law.

Compared to the concept of economic transformation, the development stages and phases can be described as the societal political transformation that lies between the collapse or overthrow of a regime and the permanent establishment of a new political order. O'Donnell/Schmitter speak of transition as the interval between one political regime and another. Under these circumstances, the two authors consider the regime to be an ensemble of explicit or implicit patterns that determine the forms and channels of access to key governmental positions, the characteristics of the actors who are excluded or have access to it the resources or strategies they can use to gain access.[36)]

To be effective, the patterns that define an existing regime must be habitually known, practiced, and accepted, at least by those who define those patterns as participants in that process.

36) O' Donnell, Guillermo and Philippe Schmitter. 1986. Transitions from Authoritarian Rule: Tentative Conclusions about Uncertain Democracies. Baltimore: Johns Hopkins University Press.

According to Glä*β*ner, regimes can be understood as formal or informal organizations at the center of political power and their relations with society. They decide who has access to political power and what rules are in dealing with those who have no power. Unlike in the field of international relations, where "regimes" are understood as principles, norms, rules and procedures of decision-making that actors agree on in a particular context, the term has a pejorative meaning in terms of political orders: it stands for undemocratic, authoritarian, military or totalitarian Forms of domination by a limited, illegitimate social group. The regime collapses in the former communist countries have revived the debate on the causes and consequences of regime change.[37)]

A comprehensive, interdisciplinary approach to explain the transformation process of Central and Eastern European countries is provided by cybernetic systems theory. The difference to the described economic models, which arise under premises in firmly defined thought spaces, is that the modeling in the cybernetic system theory takes place through the integration of the specialized knowledge of different sciences. The subject of investigation is complex systems, whose [...] analogies are to be understood in structure, structure and behavior. The systems consist of individual, interconnected elements. If one element

---

37) Glae*β*ner, G.J. (1994) Transition und Demokratisierung im Postkommunismus, Opladen

of the system is affected, it also affects the other elements of the system.[38)]

Control loops between the individual elements of a system is due to the great fault tolerance of systems. They ensure that extraneous disturbances are absorbed and, to a certain extent, compensated or integrated without intervention by the system environment. In other words, deviations from the system trigger feedback to restore the previous state. The more stable systems are, the greater their ability to neutralize extraneous disturbances through negative feedbacks or to keep the system stable (e.g., development of a low pressure vortex). If a system does not exhibit a stationary state, it removes itself auto-catalytically(self-accelerating) by positive feedback from the respective state. This development inevitably leads to the collapse of the system (e.g., uncontrolled combustion processes).[39)]

From a cybernetic-systems-theoretical point of view, system-inherent misdirections within the socialist system and its subsystems led to the collapse of the system. Since in the socialist system negative, system-stabilizing feedbacks (elections, consumer sovereignty) were not possible, it increasingly left the state of equilibrium and thus disintegrated itself. With the be-

38) Kühne, Olaf: Transformation und kybernetische Systemtheorie, in: Osteuropa Zeitschrift für Gegenwartsfragen des Ostens, Stuttgart 2001, Heft 2, [Transformation and Cybernetic Systems Theory, in: Osteuropa Zeitschrift für Gegenwartsfragen des Osten] p. 148-170.

39) Kühne, Olaf, ibid.

ginning of the transformation process, the socialist system structure dissolved itself? in favor of a democratically-market-based system with functional differentiation of the merged systems of politics, economy and socioculture as well as their subsystems. Feedback mechanisms between the individual elements of the systems and subsystems as well as their environment became possible, induced a constant learning process of all involved actors and supported the transformation process. A system characterized by linear dependencies of the micro and meso level on the macro level has been superseded by a networked, democratic market system with circular dependencies of the systems and subsystems.[40)]

3. Conclusion

The concrete definition of the term "transformation" varies with the methodological position, the problem dimension and more generally with the sociological subdiscipline. In the various socio-scientific disciplines, the term "transformation" is often defined differently: "In economics, this refers to the transition from a planned to a market economy, whereas the term in political science refers to changes in the political system.

40) Kühne, Olaf, ibid.

While a clear definition of the term does not seem to be possible without prejudice, what is generally understood as transformation in terms of the transformation of Eastern European social systems is fundamentally uncontroversial. In the process, terms such as transformation, system change and transition are used as synonyms in specialist literature.[41)]

In order to search for the development of economic and social systems in the transformation economies, the evolutionary theoretical approach is introduced, which lends itself to an objective scientific examination of the question of development processes and their explanation in the social field. Under the evolutionary theory approach, there are two different directions. On the one hand, movements that follow certain laws are recognizable in history. From this it is concluded that future social events can be planned, predicted and thus calculated. This assertion sees man's activities primarily in his reaction to the inevitable development that he can foresee based on his knowledge and thus adapt accordingly.

On the other hand, the very freedom that allows people to think and want leads to people being able to plan, set standards, realize intentions, and thus create and shape societal

41) Boxberger, Gerald: Sozialpolitik und Transformationsprozesse: Kosten der polnischen Transformation und ihre Minderung ueber staatliche Sozialpolitik und Selbsthilfeinitiativen, Frankfurt am Main, 1997, S. 17. Social Policy and Transformation Processes: Cost of Polish Transformation and its Reduction on State Social Policy and Self-Help Initiatives.

forms. These approaches differ in the assessment of the role of humans in societal development processes. These views primarily consider man as the initiator and designer of social events, which, however, can hardly be predicted, because people's thinking and actions are not determinable due to the different socio-political constellations in which they develop.[42)]

Against this evolutionary background, an attempt is made to explain the important approaches of transformation theory in order to better understand the transformation of the socialist countries. The theories of transformation have the task to clarify from which constraints, under which conditions, how and if and when such a transformation comes into question.

---

42) Paraskewopoulos, S. (1991), Erklärungsansätze der Systemtransformation, in: Hartwig, K.-H. und H.-J. Thieme (Hg.), Transformationsprozesse in sozialistischen Wirtschaftssystemen. Ursachen, Konzepte, Instrumente, Berlin, Explanation of the system transformation, in: Hartwig, K.-H. and H.-J. Thieme (ed.), Transformation Processes in Socialist Economic Systems. Causes, concepts, instruments, Berlin pp. 3-27.

Chapter 3 Innovation System in Vietnam

I. Country Profile and Historical Characteristics

With 330,000 km2, Vietnam has a similar size to Germany. The majority of the population lives in the fertile areas around the delta of the Red River in the north and the Mekong Delta in the south. In the middle of the country rise wooded mountains and plateaus. In the mid-19th century, Vietnam became a French colony and part of French Indochina. France's rule ended with the defeat in the Indochina War (1946-1954). In the ensuing peace negotiations, the partition of Vietnam was decided. This led to the outbreak of the Vietnam War (1955-1975), which began as a civil war between the communist north and the anticommunist south. From 1964, the US provided significant military support to the South, yet the North won the war in 1975. A year later, the country was reunited. Vietnam has been in a process of transformation since 1986 in a process of transformation, with the Communist Party continuing to hold on to its monopoly of power. Through its opening and renewal policies, the country has made remarkable achievements. Hand in hand with the economic boom, progress is being made in poverty reduction. While in 1996 53% of the population lived below the national poverty line, in 2010 it was only 20%.

Vietnam seeks to transform into a knowledge-based economy and society. To this end, the government offers corresponding incentives and invests, for example, in the following projects[1]:

- Manufacture of high-tech, biotechnological or information technology products
- Manufacture of industrial manufactured mechanical products
- Breeding of livestock and crops
- High technology research and use of modern technologies
- Technology Transfer.

In the context of special zones such as business parks, export trade zones, economic zones and high-tech zones, companies are granted further benefits. These zones are spread throughout Vietnam and are being marketed both in Vietnam and abroad to attract further investment. Because these zones are usually located outside metropolitan areas and thus the labor shortage is striking, the acquisition of skilled workers and the training of potential workers is now an integral part of these zones. Correspondingly, educational institutions are set up in these zones and workers are recruited at an early stage.

1) iMOVE ibid.

In addition, the establishment of high-tech zones and the creation of corresponding centers will be supported by a separate national program until 2020.[2)]

II. Political Development

The form of government of Vietnam is the one-party system. The party is the Communist Party of Vietnam (KPV) with 2.8 million members. A separation of powers is not provided for in the 1992 Vietnamese constitution. Vietnam is divided into 63 provinces, of which 58 are area provinces. The five provinces of Hanoi, Da Nang, Ho Chi Minh City, Can Tho and Haiphong are independent municipalities.[3)]

Economic power is unevenly distributed across regions: 60% of the population lives in rural areas and generates only 20% of national income, while the inhabitants of Ho Chi Minh City (HCMC) make up one tenth of the total population and one third of the gross domestic product (GDP) generate. In 2010, HCMC's residents earned $ 104 million per capita income of $ 1,260.[4)]

---

2) iMOVE ibid.

3) iMOVE beim Bundesinstitut für Berufsbildung (BIBB), Marktstudie Vietnam für den Export beruflicher Aus- und Weiterbildung, 2012

4) iMOVE beim Bundesinstitut für Berufsbildung (BIBB), Marktstudie Vietnam für den Export beruflicher Aus- und Weiterbildung, 2012

Background and Causes of Political Innovation in Vietnam

Background of Political Innovation in Vietnam

Vietnam' s political innovation began under the conditions of internal and external troubles. After undergoing major events such as resisting law, resisting Japan, building a nation, re-defending law, resisting the United States, and unifying North and South Vietnam, the Vietnamese economy has not developed, and the country' s reunification broke out again. In the economic crisis, the change in the Soviet Union's Eastern dramas has added to the political pressure on the ruling Communist Party of Vietnam. However, during the same period of China' s reform and opening up, it is becoming increasingly popular and contrasting with the Soviet Union' s Eastern European countries.

Domestic background

The historical background of Vietnam's reform and opening up has to be a French colonial search since modern times. In June 1858, France and the Spanish Navy Fleet shelled the central port of Toulon (present-day Danang City) in Central Vietnam and opened the process of colonial Vietnam. In 1884, the then-ruling dynasty government of Vietnam was forced to sign a surrender treaty with the French colonists, formally acknowledging that France was a protectorate of Vietnam. In this colonial context, in February 1930, when the Communist Party of Vietnam was established in Hong Kong and was renamed the Communist Party of Indochina in October of that year, the Vietnamese Communist Party took Vietnam as its main pursuit from the beginning of its establishment. In September 1940, Japan became a new colonizer of Vietnam. In May 1941, the Vietnam Democratic League was established under the leadership of the Communist Party of Indochina. Under the leadership of the Vietnam Democratic League, the Vietnamese people not only defeated the Japanese invaders, but also overthrew the feudal autocratic system of nearly a thousand years. In August 1945, the Democratic Republic of Vietnam was established. However, France invaded Vietnam again. In 1951, the Communist Party of Indochina was renamed the Vietnam Labor Party. In July 1954, the War of Resistance Against Japan won, and the entire territory of Vietnam began to divide by 17 degrees north and south, gradually forming a northern Vietnam. The Democratic Republic and the Republic of Vietnam in the South are two countries. Afterwards, the United States began to invade Vietnam and support the South Vietnamese government. On April 30, 1975, the Vietnamese People' s Army captured the capital of South Vietnam' s regime, Saigon (present-day Ho Chi Minh City). The final victory was achieved in the War of Resistance against Americans and Saving the Nation, and the

North and South of Vietnam finally achieved unity. In 1976, the name of Vietnam changed from the Democratic Republic of Vietnam to the Socialist Republic of Vietnam, and the Vietnamese Labor Party was renamed the Communist Party of Vietnam. Since the establishment of the Twelfth National Congress in February 1930 and held in January 2016, the Vietnamese Communist Party has passed. From the period of 86 years of armed struggle to innovation and opening up, there are about 4.5 million current members.[5]

International background

In 1917, Lenin' s October Socialist Revolution won victory and established the world' s first socialist country, the Soviet Union. After the end of the Second World War, the socialist countries developed from the Soviet Union into more than 20 countries throughout Asia, Africa, and Eastern Europe. In the early days of the establishment of the political power, the political and economic development models of the socially-meaning countries in the countries of Eastern Europe and Asia-Africa, Latin America and Latin America were basically established by copying or mimicking the Soviet Union model. In the process of socialist construction, various countries have gradually discovered the problem of the Soviet Union model, and there

5) Guocao, The Political System Reform in Vietnam and Its Implications, 2016

have been strong calls for the reform of the political and economic system and their own road of socialist development. After the 20th National Congress of the CPSU in 1956, Poland and Hungary first launched the reforms that opposed the Soviet Union's control and emerged from the Soviet Union model. In the middle of the 1960s, the socialist countries in eastern Europe set off a climax of reforms. After nearly a decade of exploration and practice under the leadership of Qatar, Hungary implemented a new economic management system and greatly improved the level of economic development. In the 1980s, due to the influence of the "new thinking" of Gorbachev' s reform of the General Secretary of the Communist Party of the Soviet Union, Bulgaria, Hungary, Czechoslovakia, Poland, Democratic Germany and other socialist countries in the former Soviet Union' s Eastern Europe region successively promoted democracy. Reforms. However, these reforms failed to save the ruling Communist Party and the socialist regime. In the late 1980s and early 1990s, the Communist Party that had been in power for more than half a century lost leadership in these countries. The wave of reforms in these socialist countries has played an external role in promoting Vietnam' s reforms. In particular, the drastic changes in the Soviet Union and East Europe have caused great shock to the leadership of the Vietnamese Communist Party.[6)]

---

6) Guocao, The Political System Reform in Vietnam and Its Implications, 2016

China implemented reform and opening up earlier and thus became the first example of innovation in Vietnam.

Reasons for Political Innovation in Vietnam

There are similarities in the reasons for the implementation of political innovation and economic reform in Vietnam, because the old Soviet model has been difficult to sustain and must be changed. Viet Nam's truly full implementation of political innovation is basically 10 years after the economic reform. At that time, the political system has become an obstacle to the continued deepening of economic innovation. Moreover, the "national disaster" of corruption has been deeply integrated into the bone marrow of the Vietnamese Communists, causing great dissatisfaction among the Vietnamese people. They are gradually demanding greater opportunities and the right to speak in the management of state affairs. This growing demand for democracy Virtually there has been a strong pressure on the Central Committee of the Communist Party of Vietcong, forcing the Vietnamese Communist Party to fully implement the reform of the political system.[7)]

1) The need for further development of economic innovation
2) The people' s democratic demands gradually increase

7) Guocao, The Political System Reform in Vietnam and Its Implications, 2016

3) The corruption issue is seriously undermining political innovation

4) The promotion of the wave of democratization in the world

III. Economic Transformation and Innovation System

1. Economic transformation

Since the economic opening to a "socialist market economy" as part of the "Doi Moi" reform in 1986, Vietnam has experienced a continuous economic upswing with growth rates of 7% on average. The country recovered comparatively quickly from the economic and financial crisis in 2009, not least due to government stimulus packages, which amount to around 8,5% of GDP with a volume of 8 billion USD.[8)]

As part of the membership of the WTO reforms were announced in the state enterprises, but not yet fully implemented. From around 12,000 state-owned enterprises in 1989, the number fell to around 1,500 in 2011, and its share of economic output halved from 60% in 2000 to 30% in 2011. However, these state-owned companies still have 60 to 70% of their natural and

8) iMOVE beim Bundesinstitut für Berufsbildung (BIBB), Marktstudie Vietnam für den Export beruflicher Aus- und Weiterbildung, 2012

financial resources. Especially in the key areas of coal, oil and gas, electricity and chemicals and fertilizers dominate the state-owned enterprises. At present, 34 state-owned enterprises belong to the group of 50 companies with the highest turnover nationwide. Nine of them are even among the "Top Ten".[9)]

Economic structure and perspectives

Vietnam, the sixth largest economy in Southeast Asia, offers many potentials. Entrepreneurship and a consumer-friendly middle class have been developing dynamically since the 1986 opening up. The positive outlook, cheap labor and political stability attract foreign investors. The socialist state wants to make the leap to modern industrialized countries by 2020. This requires profound reforms. Since 2008, the economy has been following a path with growth rates of 5.2% to 6.4%. Reforms of the financial sector, a reduction in the protection of state-owned companies and more efficient public investment could lead to a significantly higher growth rate. As the government implements a "market economy with a socialist orientation," it is deeply involved in some areas of the economy. State-owned corporate groups are specifically preferred, land is public property. Large parts of the country continue to be underdeveloped. Here investors receive particularly attractive

9) iMOVE ibid.

subsidies from the state. While the South focuses on a private-sector, export-oriented light industry (including apparel, electronics, wood furniture manufacturing) and business-related services (including finance, outsourcing), state-owned companies are focused on the north.[10)]

Investment climate and risks

Foreign investors appreciate Vietnam and their direct investments are flowing steadily. However, the country must increasingly compete in regional competition against countries such as China, Thailand or Cambodia. In the long run cheap labor will no longer suffice as the most important location factor of Vietnam. In order to attract more sophisticated investment, the state is seeking higher levels of education and technology, as well as more efficient use of resources. Vietnam's advantages over other Asian locations include, among other things, the low risk of expropriation, political stability and a relatively low tax burden. Location disadvantages include corruption, bureaucracy, education and higher education as well as the quality of the infrastructure. The amount of the promised capital values of the investors fluctuates strongly from year to year. However, since

10) Deutsche Gesellschaft für Internationale Zusammenarbeit (GIZ) GmbH(ed.) Vietnam, Neue Märkte - Neue Chancen, Ein Wegweiser für deutsche Unternehme, 2016

2008 foreign direct investment has been very stable at between $ 10 billion and $ 11.5 billion per year.[11)]

Energy and Renewable Energy

Vietnam's electricity demand is growing at double-digit rates. The capacity expansion, however, hardly keeps pace with this. Investments are mainly directed towards coal or gas power plants and the pipeline network to stabilize supply. Although the state has recognized the potential of renewable energies, the subsidized electricity prices are still too low for a breakthrough. The country's electricity needs are expected to increase by 12 to 13% annually by 2020. The national utility Electricity of Vietnam (EVN) expects electricity generation of 142 TW in 2015 with a total installed capacity of 34 GW. Capacity expansion has been a big leap in the last ten years, with only 11.6 GW installed in 2005. At present, about 35% of the capacity is accounted for by water, 32% by coal and 18% by gas-fired power plants. The rest are oil power plants, renewable energies and electricity imports.[12)]

---

11) Deutsche Gesellschaft für Internationale Zusammenarbeit (GIZ) GmbH(ed.), ibid.

12) Deutsche Gesellschaft für Internationale Zusammenarbeit (GIZ) GmbH(ed.), ibid.

Chemistry and Chemical Industry

Vietnam provides chemical companies with fast-growing, import-dependent markets. A local industry is still under construction, refineries and major petrochemical projects are planned. Foreign companies also invest locally. The emerging market must import many raw materials and end products, most of which are supplied by the PRC. Since domestic customers mainly ask for cheap chemicals, German quality products need convincing. International buyers, however, certainly ask for quality, environmental compatibility and sustainability. Sales of fertilizers are steadily increasing. Agriculture consumed about 10.3 million tonnes in 2013, of which 4.7 million tonnes were imported - mainly from the PRC. About 19,000 t came from Germany.The Ministry of Agriculture estimates that the market reached around 11 million tonnes in 2014. Farmers and agricultural companies are increasingly using crop protection products. In 2013, insecticides amounted to $ 786 million, half of which came from the PRC. Local companies mix the materials for the specific needs of the farmers. The German Bayer AG operates two factories in which active ingredients for plant protection products are formulated. Other providers include Syngenta, DuPont, BASF and Dow. The food processing industry and the beverage industry are also thriving.[13)]

13) Deutsche Gesellschaft für Internationale Zusammenarbeit (GIZ) GmbH(ed.), ibid.

German Association for International Cooperation (GIZ) GmbH (ed.) Vietnam, New Markets - New Opportunities, A Guide for German Companies, 2016

Mechanical and plant engineering

Vietnam's demand for engineering products is booming. Sectoral imports increased by around a third in the first half of 2015. As customers tend to lower priced machines, German equipment has played only a small role in the standard segment so far. However, financially strong customers are increasingly providing efficient, technically precise German equipment, which enjoys a high reputation in Vietnam. Germany supplies mainly power plant or conveyor technology as well as packaging machines. Large customer industries such as the automotive industry, metalworking or local mechanical engineering are still lacking in breadth. A tight distribution network and a nationwide after-sales service are essential for business success.[14)]

2. Innovation System

Vietnam is constantly advancing reforms in science and research, away from the old, socialist to more modern, more open structures. Each year, about 1 million young people in

14) Deutsche Gesellschaft für Internationale Zusammenarbeit (GIZ) GmbH(ed.), ibid.

Vietnam seek their entry into the labor market. Despite this large number of new workers, there is also a shortage of skilled workers in Vietnam. This is partly due to the positive economic development. On the other hand, only very few young people have a post-school education.[15]

Education System

With the opening of the market in Vietnam, education was also liberalized. In addition to state educational offers, a growing number of private educational institutions is emerging, partly in the form of international cooperation and participation. State responsibilities have been redefined and several comprehensive reforms launched.

The literacy rate of 93% reflects the educational achievements in primary education. At the same time, especially children in rural areas drop out of education after elementary school, because their parents can not afford the necessary tuition. Among young employees, about 40% enjoyed post-school education. However, only 13% of the working-age population have completed vocational training.[16]

15) iMOVE ibid.
16) iMOVE ibid.

school-system

The Vietnamese school system is uniformly structured nationwide. It starts with the nursery for children up to 3 years or the kindergarten for children from 3 years. There, the alphabet is already taught. At the age of 6, the children start the five-year elementary school.

The junior high school lasts four years, from the sixth to the ninth grade. Certificates are issued for the first time at the end of ninth grade and for the entire period at the middle school. They are the basis for the decision to attend high school or to start vocational training.[17)]

Prerequisites for attending a secondary school are central entrance examinations, for which the respective "Office for Education and Training" is responsible. Private high schools and gifted institutions conduct their entrance examinations themselves. The three-year secondary school is completed with the Abitur.[18)]

---

17) Socialist Republic of Vietnam(2011a): Action Program to implement the Vietnamese Human resource development strategy during 20112020. Online: http://english.molisa.gov.vn/Default. aspx?tabid=345&temidclicked=469

18) Socialist Republic of Vietnam(2011a), ibid.

training

Vietnam's VET system includes three types of VET, which differ in terms of access criteria, duration of offers and completion options: vocational centers, vocational schools and vocational colleges.

The focus of the vocational centers are short training courses with a duration of 3 to 12 months. In a sequence of several modules but also courses over longer periods, up to one and a half years, carried out. The offer is intended to meet the needs of the local economy and is aimed at school and college graduates as well as professionals.[19)]

The first vocational centers were founded in the 1990s. There are no general professional admission requirements. However, the qualifications of vocational centers are not considered qualifications for access to vocational schools or vocational colleges. Training at vocational schools takes 2 to 3 years. The vocational schools train skilled workers. There are full-time vocational schools and "technical vocational schools", which also include subjects of upper secondary school. A degree from a technical vocational school enables the transition to the university, to the technical high school or to the vocational

19) iMOVE ibid.

college. However, graduating from a full-time vocational school allows you to attend a vocational college only.[20)]

The highest vocational training levels are offered by the vocational colleges. Here, a distinction is made between "educational vocational colleges" for the education of primary school teachers, "medical vocational colleges" for the training of nurses above the nursing profession and "technical vocational colleges" with offers in the areas of economics, finance, culture and arts and crafts. Entry requirement is the central entrance examination. Graduation from a vocational college allows students to study or a visit to the Fachgymnasiale Oberstufe.[21)]

In Vietnam, there are far more applications than places available both at universities and at VET institutions. As a rule, there are 2 to 3 applications for an apprenticeship position. Those who do not find a training place usually apply to other vocational training institutions, sign up for training courses that are not part of the regular training modules, or seek a job as an unskilled worker.[22)]

---

20) iMOVE ibid.
21) iMOVE ibid.
22) iMOVE ibid.

Chapter 4 Innovation System in Indonesia

I. Country Profile and Historical Characteristics

The Republic of Indonesia, with about 255 million inhabitants, is one of the most populous countries in the world and has a great ethnic and cultural diversity. The national territory extends as an island chain about 5,000 km. Of the more than 17,000 islands in the country, about 6,000 are inhabited. The climate is tropical with temperatures of mostly 25-35 ° C. Indonesia was once part of the Dutch colonial empire and declared independence in 1945. In 1965, Major General Suharto took over the government of Indonesia and he directed an authoritarian rule. In his 32-year term of office, human rights were massively disregarded. In 1998, in the wake of the Asian economic crisis, serious social unrest resulted in Suharto's resignation. Since then Indonesia has been in a process of political and economic transformation. Democracy is considered relatively stable today, and the presidential elections of 2014 went smoothly. The national economy is also developing dynamically. The newly industrializing country is a member of the G20 group and plays a leading role in the Association of

Southeast Asian Nations ASEAN. However, many challenges remain, such as corruption or the lack of capacity of state institutions.[1)]

Indonesia's demographic, political and economic center is located on the island of Java, which accounts for only seven percent of Indonesia's land mass, but home to just over half of Indonesia's approximately 240 million people. Here lies the capital Jakarta, a dynamic, pulsating metropolis of vertiginous contrasts of bitter poverty next to glittering megamalls with an estimated 10 million inhabitants. In Jabodetabek, as the rapidly expanding metropolitan area of the cities of Jakarta, Bogor, Depok, Tangerang and Bekasi is called, over 22 million people live. Java also has four out of five cities in Indonesia with over two million inhabitants. More than 60 percent of Indonesia's gross domestic product is generated in Java alone.[2)]

Indonesia has had significant regional disparities since the Dutch colonial era: with regard to demographic development, economic development, infrastructure, and the education and health sectors, there is a significant imbalance between Java as the center of Indonesia and the periphery, the so-called "outer islands". When Suharto fell in the course of the Asian crisis in

---

1) German Trade & Invest (Ed.), Indonesia, New Markets - New Opportunities, A Guide for German Entrepreneurs, April 2016

2) Bettina David, Shifts of Power Between Indonesia's Center and Periphery, in: From Politics and Contemporary History, Volume 62, 11-12, 2012

1998 and the era of reformasi, the political reform process, was initiated, the ambitious project of the political reorganization of Indonesia, particularly in the peripheral regions outside Java, had high hopes for a policy that would be regional Differences and takes into account the ethnic diversity of the multinational state.[3)]

The beginnings of civil society life in Indonesia go back to the Dutch colonial era, when local communities embraced issues such as education, social affairs and microcredit. Trade union life also began here; In addition, the founding of mass religious organizations such as Muhammadiyah (1912) and Nahdatul Ulama (1926) entered this phase. Although there is some controversy about whether religious groups are part of civil society, their often charitable and social agenda speaks for it. Another argument can be found in the debate on an adequate translation of the civil society concept into Indonesian. While masyarakat madani recalls the reign of the Prophet Muhammed about the community in Medina (umma) - a picture of the desirable democratic and liberal order - and thus an Islamic understanding of civil society, masyarat sipil stands for a secular translation.[4)]

---

3) Bettina David, 2012, ibid.

4) Marc Frings, Civil Society in Indonesia, in: From Politics and Contemporary History, Volume 62, 11-12, 2012

II. Political Development

Indonesia, the fourth largest country in the world with 220 million people, has made the breakthrough to democracy with the 2004 elections. The Indonesians made a premiere: for the first time, the president of a state with a predominantly Muslim population was directly elected. An important result is the acceptance of the new political system. The political elite showed them through peaceful election campaigns and the absence of disturbances during the ballots. Military men with political ambitions retired and stood up to democratic competition. The people showed their acceptance by high voter turnout. Within six months, about 80% of the claimants cast their votes three times. The parliamentary elections in April were followed by two presidential elections in July and September. The success is the result of a reform process that began with the overthrow of General Suharto in May 1998. Suharto had ruled for 32 years, as an autocrat he headed a centralist repressive state. The general had given his military regime a pale democracy painting, there were three parties and electoral antics. Now democratic structures are so firmly established that a return to other systems is unimaginable - for the first time since 1945, when independence was declared by the Dutch colonial power. In 2004, for the first time, Indonesians directly elected the president and appointed regional and national parliaments in which military officials no longer have guaranteed seats.[5)]

A unique three-chamber system made up of the House of Representatives (Parliament), the "Regional Representatives Council" (Regional Council) and the People's Assembly gives regions more political influence. The members of parliament are elected from party lists, the regional council even more direct, they act as independents. Both chambers together form the People's Assembly, which may change the constitution. It is scheduled to meet every five years, but may be called, for example, to vote for a replacement if the president or his vice dies. The reforms have enormously strengthened the parliament, it can theoretically pass laws against the will of the regional council and president. In practice, this is hard to imagine. Indonesia still has a presidential system. The President is Head of State and Government and Commander-in-Chief of the Armed Forces; his team designs the laws. His office has also been strengthened, he can now be relieved only with the involvement of the Constitutional Court. The system is untested and it will be immediately exciting: the strengthened president does not have a secure majority in the strengthened parliament. The executive and the legislature are currently exploring their

---

5) Moritz Kleine-Brockhoff, Indonesia: Breakthrough for Democracy, Friedrich Ebert Foundation, December 2004

limits of competence, for example in the dispute over the nomination of the "Panglima", which is the supreme general, the chief of the armed forces. Basically, the president should keep the saying for a simple reason: because he is president. In Indonesia, nothing is more important than hierarchy. Perhaps democracy will change cultural and social norms, but by no means overnight.[6)]

Looking at the place of the public in Indonesia until 1998, this was under the sole sovereignty of General Suharto. His regime combined all forms of state and military force to keep existing power relations stable. But this stability was blatantly challenged when the dictator's forced resignation in May 1998 broke his intellectual and political monopoly. The two presidents of the first Reformasi years, Jusuf Habibie (1998-1999) and Abdurrahman Wahid (1999-2001), allowed the development of a multiparty system, reintroducing civil rights, thus fertilizing the earth from which many civil society organizations grew. These met with numerous foreign organizations that were now entering Indonesia.[7)]

The laws on regional autonomy, which were swiftly passed in 1999 and implemented in 2001, aimed to strengthen the

6) Moritz Kleine-Brockhoff, 2004, ibid.

7) Marc Frings, 2012, ibid.

self-government of the regions. Since 2005, the governors of the 33 provinces, the district chiefs and mayors have also been elected in direct elections (pilkada). All this promised a policy in which no longer as in the Suharto period by politicians appointed from above or from Jakarta and close to Javanese-centralist interests have the say, but better implemented the regional interests of the local population by their directly elected government representatives can be. With consistent decentralization and the introduction of regional autonomy, the government in Jakarta sought to counteract existing (Aceh, Papua, East Timor) and potential secessionist movements in the peripheral regions, thereby preserving the territorial integrity of the multi-national state. For security reasons in particular, the peripheral provinces, some of which are extraordinarily rich in raw materials, have been given high priority since Indonesian independence in 1945.[8)]

Indonesia is rich in natural resources, especially tropical timber, oil, natural gas, copper, coal, tin and gold. Under Suharto's central-autocratic regime, the mineral wealth of the resource-rich provinces of Kalimantan (the part of Borneo belonging to Indonesia), Sumatra, and Papua was firmly in the hands of large national and international corporations working

8) Bettina David, Shifts of Power Between Indonesia's Center and Periphery, in: From Politics and Contemporary History, Volume 62, 11-12, 2012

closely with the Suharto clan, while the local population ran out and could not benefit from the abundance of natural resources in their home country. Here, the reorganization of political, administrative and financial relations between the central government in Jakarta and the regions promised stronger decision-making power at the local level and thus a fairer distribution of revenues, not only to the center of Jakarta and abroad, but finally to the local population and thus benefit the regional construction in Indonesia's periphery.[9)]

However, the first dark sides of the dynamics of regional empowerment, which had been set in motion with the decentralization process, soon became apparent. Regional autonomy has given a significant increase in power to local self-government, especially to the administrative levels of districts (kabupaten) and cities, past provincial governments. What was meant to promote locally responsible governance has all too often proved in practice to be a new arena for the struggle of local elites for control of local resources. Not infrequently, the regional "democracy" on closer inspection turns out to be money politics and thuggery. For candidacies high costs are to be estimated, without bribe hardly anything runs. Financing requires good relationships with wealthy, influential personalities and entrepreneurs - not infrequently the candidates themselves be-

9) Bettina David, 2012, ibid.

long to this group of people who now make a career in local politics and use their economic power to expand their political influence (or vice versa). This creates opaque and difficult-to-overcome clientelistic dependency relationships that oppose the democratic demands for transparency.[10]

In 2004, the election took place. Then the new parliament changed Indonesia's political culture.

70% of the parliamentarians were exchanged. More women than ever before were lined up, just as few were elected as in the past, and 90% of MEPs continue to be men. Indonesia's small women's movement sees Megawati's paleness as head of government a forgiving profiling opportunity. There was also success with President Megawati; since September 2004, marriage violence has been a crime. The new parliament is changing Indonesia's political culture, for the first time in the history of the country there is a real opposition. So far, Parliament has been a big government club. Wahid and Megawati had brought all the relevant parties by all-round allocation of Cabinet posts on the boat. The result, demonstrated long-term agreement in parliament, fulfilled socio-cultural norms. There was no opposition in the Western sense, no true debates. Opposition, rejection of any kind, is considered indecent in Indonesia. [11]

---

10) Bettina David, 2012, ibid.

11) Moritz Kleine-Brockhoff, Indonesia: Breakthrough for Democracy, Friedrich Ebert Foundation, December 2004

Of course, they are everywhere on a daily basis, but rejection is not. Instead of saying "No" you say "Yes, later". If someone exposed the weakness of his opponent in a political debate, he would have disqualified himself. He would henceforth be described as rude and reckless. Indonesian political confrontations are tough. Popular art is to hide hardness and still prevail. After the election of SBY to the president, something sensational happened: the presidential-election losers (the big parties had supported Megawati) did not want cabinet posts and formed an opposition coalition in parliament. SBY, whose party holds only 10% of the seats, could only seek support from the small, Islamic parties. He did that, so a loose coalition government emerged, with the SBY at best 40% of the deputies behind him. The first weeks of the session were spent by the parliamentarians only with a dispute over the nomination of committee chairmen and their deputies. In the process, the dominant opposition prevailed without compromise. In the long term, especially in direct power trials with the executive, elephant behavior is dangerous to the government. SBY is likely to become popular with the people. Those who constantly blockade opposition risks losing popularity and splitting their own party.[12)]

---

12) Moritz Kleine-Brockhoff, 2004, ibid.

Since 1998, a stable multi-party system has developed in Indonesia. Nine parties succeeded in entering the national parliament in the 2009 elections. However, these can not be categorized according to Western criteria in "conservative", "left" or "green". An anti-democratic party is not represented in parliament. Despite the decentralized anchoring with branches in all provinces, the parties often lack internal democratic structures. According to a research team, because of allegations of corruption, poor legislative performance and lack of communication, civil society in parliament and parties primarily sees the "bad side of democracy". In addition, according to an Indonesian NGO representative, access to public space is handled variably by the way of the parties: at any rate, this is explained by the ongoing debate about raising the threshold for the next parliamentary election in 2014, which currently stands at 2.5 percent lies. This should manifest the power of the parties currently represented in parliament and prevent the success of new movements.[13)]

This contributes significantly to the fact that civil society, while praising the role of the parties as pillars of democracy, keeps as much as possible a skeptical distance to them. The structural and content issues of the parties and their negative

---

13) Marc Frings, 2012, ibid.

image within civil society currently prevent cooperation between the two groups. From the above described, socio-political bridging function of the Indonesian parties can be spoken only conditionally therefore at present. Ultimately, this makes it harder for civil society to influence politics because it is self-critical that it has only insufficient influence on the parliamentary process. NGOs see the cooperation with the ministries as more promising. The organizations profit from the fact that they have no direct party political influence, so that they can directly transfer knowledge. The ministerial working level is open and constructive for this expertise. From a strategic perspective, lobbying for a decision on a substance does not take place in the parliamentary committees, but rather late, in the executive branch.[14)]

The importance of a vibrant civil society, understood as the engine of political change, can not be overstated for the success of a democratization process. Its permanent public presence is considered a barometer of stable democracy, provided that it acts free of political interference "from above". At the same time, it is up to the respective rulers to define the civil society room for maneuver, which determines the relationship between the citizens on the one hand and the state power on

14) Marc Frings, 2012, ibid.

the other. Civil society as a precondition for democracy requires the existence of comprehensive liberties such as freedom of expression, speech, press and assembly in order to be able to develop effectively. Only when they do exist can a civil society become a constructive "countervailing force" in the extra-parliamentary space, which points politics to other, mostly marginalized, issues and social strata and suggests solutions.[15)]

Their organizational design can be manifold. Trade unions and associations are just as much part of this as are spontaneous and short-term mass and protest movements. There are also academic research institutes, media and social organizations. The most prominent form of organization is the non-governmental organization (NGO).

The term NGO emphasizes the distance to institutionalized politics - a dividing line that, however, is dwindling in times of political co-optation. Political parties can not be counted among civil society, as they seek, among other things, the acquisition of political power. However, as intermediary actors, they form a bridge from society to the formal political process and vice versa, which is why they are taken into consideration below. Although the civil society model emerged against the back-

---

15) Marc Frings, 2012, ibid.

ground of Western democratization processes, many characteristics have been confirmed as universal. However, cultural, regional and historical features have to be considered. The majority assume that civil society is accompanied by a normative catalog of values based on global human rights discourse. This is incomplete in that organizations with anti-democratic or anti-democratic positions can also be part of civil society.[16)]

Since 2006, Indonesia has been awarded the title "free" by the US think tank Freedom House, a leading institute for measuring democracy and political freedoms, and is thus at the top of the Southeast Asian countries in terms of its democratic performance. This paper explores the evolution of Indonesian civil society since the country's independence from the Dutch colonial power. It shows that she has always succeeded in adapting to the respective political and social limits of movement. Today, it is largely subject to trends that are comparatively also found in other so-called developing and emerging countries. This includes the double challenge of civil society to find and maintain its own place in the post-authoritarian order, as well as to carry out internal adaptations in order to meet the current (development) political rules of the game. Furthermore, Indonesia is suitable for sketching exemplary cul-

---

16) Marc Frings, 2012, ibid.

tural and regional peculiarities of civil society genesis. Dominant factors for this were the specific points of contact with the Dutch colonial administration and authoritarian rule until 1998.[17)]

Indonesia's history is a story of conflict. Under Suharto they were suppressed by military force. After the end of the Suharto era, conflicts between various religious and ethnic groups spread rapidly. There are also cases of conflict within ethnic and religious groups, but they have been labeled differently, such as the war between practitioners of black magic in East Java.

The murders of local leaders in East Java between 1998 and 1999, referred to in public as "the black magic war", the conflict between Dayak's and Madurian immigrants in Kalimantan, the conflict between religious groups in central Sulawesi, the conflict between tribal groups in West Papua , the conflict between religious groups in the Moluccas and in the northern part of the Moluccas: they all broke out after major investments had been made in the region. Kalimantan was prepared for coal mining and large plantations. In Central Sulawesi, there are three major transnational and four national corporations

---

17) Marc Frings, 2012, ibid.

planning to expand their operations in nickel, gold, oil and gas mining, palm growing and electricity generation. East Java is about to become a new oil field and a testing ground for genetically modi fi ed seeds of transnational agricultural corporations. All these activities need the land that belongs to the local population, which is why the latter was expelled from their land.[18)]

This is common to all so-called horizontal conflicts (ie ethnic, religious and conflict between other groups) in Indonesia. They all broke out after new investment or expansion of existing investments. Conflicts exist only where there is an abundance of natural resources that can be exploited by large national and transnational corporations. In their book "Multitude," Antontio Negri and Michael Hardt point to the relationships between global interests, multinational corporations, and local conflicts, such as in Aceh. The new slogan of reconciliation processes in many conflict areas is: "Conflict - No, Investment - Yes!" This is presented to the local population as if "investments" were a new religion or ethnicity that people have to adopt as an alternative to their previous religion or ethnicity. The local population is faced with the confinement or takeover of their traditional land ownership by multinational or national corporations.

---

18) Don K. Marut, Local Autonomy: Community Initiatives for Sustainable Peace, in: Country Profile Indonesia, 2007

Those who fight for their land are referred to as masterminds of conflict or are stigmatized as "provocateurs".[19)]

Experts and practitioners in the field of participatory development assume that knowledge is created through association and communication. In communities with strong social and cultural links, knowledge has been constructed, transmitted, developed and even sanctioned across generations. As a part of higher knowledge one calls moral values, which are developed to rules and norms, which regulate thought and behavior patterns. This type of knowledge becomes norms, rules, institutions, and values that serve the community as a moral foundation, cultural guidance, and belief.[20)]

Moral foundations and cultural orientation aids serve to form opinions and to make collectively binding decisions, both for the entire community and for individual family groups, households and individuals. In addition, they determine patterns of behavior and interaction between members of the community and between members of their own and other communities.[21)]

In terms of conflict, the world view also determines whether the community as a whole is called to collectively engage in

19) Don K. Marut, 2007, ibid.
20) Don K. Marut, 2007, ibid.
21) Don K. Marut, 2007, ibid.

conflict, or whether this is an individual responsibility. The levels of responsibility in collective actions are also determined by the social and moral foundations. There are only two reasons in the Moluccas that mobilize the community to participate collectively in confrontational conflicts: land and sea borders and women. In violation of the land and sea borders, the whole community participates in their defense. Measures range from peaceful approaches such as negotiations to open warfare.[22)]

When a woman in the community is harassed by a man outside the community, it also commits the community to collective action. Land and sea are perceived as the main basis of existence. Therefore, the rules for the use of land and sea and the rules for the protection of lands are well developed and strong. Women are perceived as the source of human life, so the harassment of a woman is interpreted as a disregard for the origin of all life. Religion is not seen by the people of the Moluccas as an occasion for collective action, but rather as an external factor and as an individual theme. A disregard of religion accordingly does not commit to collective action. Thus, the alleged religious or ethnic conflicts are mainly due to external factors. The media often referred to the presence of external "provocateurs" in the conflicts that disappeared after stirring up unrest and conflict.[23)]

---

22) Don K. Marut, 2007, ibid.

III. Economic Transformation and Innovation System

1. Economic transformation

President Sukarno (1945-1967) took up the social participation in the process of building up independent Indonesia during the first years of government. From the "steered democracy" (1959) and at the latest in the "New Order" under General Suharto (1967-1998), the social component had to give way to a purely economically thought-through development approach. Political participation rights were curtailed, mass organizations banned, the media placed under state surveillance and the party system limited to three forces. The first years of independence, when, for example, unions and students were still able to participate in the political process, came to a brief democracy experiment between the colonial (external) and the 1959 authoritarian (internal) occupation of public space. The suppression of social participation demands in Indonesia by the authoritarian regime corresponded to political developments throughout the Southeast Asian region.[24)]

Deprived of their political instincts, NGOs stood up to the "New Order" by adapting to Suharto's developmental paradigm and leaping into the gaps of its economic policies. So-called

---

23) Don K. Marut, 2007, ibid.

24) Marc Frings, 2012, ibid.

development NGOs focused their work from the 1970s on marginalized groups of the impoverished lower class. The pressure to adapt catapulted the NGOs into an apolitical space, but at the same time provided them with a survival strategy. An aftermath emptied the political systematic persecution of communists following the failed coup attempt of 1965. As a result of rampant anti-communism, the political left was weakened and largely banned from the public.[25)]

Contrary to the modernization theory assumption that the chance of successful democratization grows with the prosperity of a society, Suharto succeeded in achieving economic success while co-opting and marginalizing crucial veto powers. This did not change in the 1980s, when the global sprouting of environmental issues, also due to conflicts over land in the periphery, took hold in Indonesia. Advocacy NGOs, which emerged as a new NGO category and soon took on other topics, continued to adhere to the dictates of political restraint.[26)]

Glasnost in Indonesian: 1998 and the consequences

A paradigm shift did not set in until the 1990s, when despite legal and political repressions human rights violations denounced and democratic reforms were increasingly demanded.

25) Marc Frings, 2012, ibid.
26) Marc Frings, 2012, ibid.

Limited liberalization (keterbukaan), introduced in the late 1980s but withdrawn in 1994, empowered the critical sections of civil society in their struggle for change. Regarding the relevance of the latter in the fall of Suharto in 1998, the assessments differ: Although the student protests, the role of the media and the introduction of the reform discourse are appreciated as a merit, many observers are more decisive than the Asian crisis of 1997. It was the immense socio-economic consequences of the inflation and mass poverty in the broader society. As a result, the successive occupation of political issues by civil society should not be underestimated. It was this change of consciousness that made citizens take to the streets for both socio-economic and political change.[27)]

Economic structure and perspectives

Indonesia, by far the largest economy in Southeast Asia, is experiencing a long-lasting and continuous growth phase. Between 2004 and 2014, real economic growth averaged almost 6%. The archipelago is not a classic emerging economy with a broad-based and export-oriented industry. In 2014, manufacturing accounted for only 21% of GDP. Indonesia lives from its huge natural resources. The country has large deposits of natural gas, coal and mineral ores. The mining sector, including the

27) Marc Frings, 2012, ibid.

oil and gas sectors, accounted for nearly 10% of GDP in 2014. In addition, the country has huge plantations and 2014 was the largest palm oil and the second most important exporter of rubber in the world. The construction sector has also developed into another important economic pillar in recent years - the outdated and undersized infrastructure is being expanded for a great deal of money. The metropolitan area of Jakarta as well as the neighboring West Javanese areas are the economic center of the country. Over 90% of all company headquarters are located in this bacon belt. Since 2014, the Indonesian government has pursued a strong protectionist policy to protect the domestic economy from competition.[28)]

Investment climate and risks

Indonesia has been politically stable since the return to democracy in 1998. Public debt is low and political and financial stability is accompanied by a buoyant economy. According to AC Nielsen, Indonesia was the second most attractive consumer goods market in the world in 2014. Wages have risen sharply as a result of the upturn. Thus, the statutory minimum wages in the Greater Jakarta area reached the equivalent of $ 200 a month in 2015. Foreign companies on the ground complain

---

28) German Trade & Invest (Ed.), Indonesia, New Markets - New Opportunities, A Guide for German Entrepreneurs, April 2016

above all about rampant corruption and an escalating bureaucracy. In addition, they have to live with constantly changing legal framework conditions: New regulations are issued regularly, but old ones are not annulled. It is unclear to what extent the laws are actually implemented and whether companies can sue for their rights. The so-called "Negative Investment List" regulates the sectors in which international companies are allowed to invest and which shares. All international companies are as it were affected by these risks, which they price accordingly in their products. Imported goods in Jakarta cost about 25% more than in Singapore, which has positive effects on profit and margin. Hardly any entrepreneur complains meanwhile about problems in the protection of intellectual property.[29)]

The economy of Indonesia has experienced a rapid rise since the Asian crisis of the late 1990s. According to the World Bank, gross domestic product per capita increased from $ 857 in 2000 to $ 3,603 in 2016. Since 1999, the poverty rate has halved to 10.9 percent in 2016. With real GDP growth of 4.7 percent to 6.3 percent a year since 2004, G20 member Indonesia is considered the largest economy in the region and the world's tenth largest in terms of purchasing power. A wealth of natural re-

29) German Trade & Invest (Ed.), 2016, ibid.

sources and the growing guarantee of political stability, as well as a more investment-friendly economic policy of the current government, especially in the last three years, are creating a positive economic development.[30)]

However, the current weakness of the global economy has also left its mark on the Indonesian economy. The strong growth of the first decade of the millennium has noticeably declined since 2011. Low commodity prices and the uncertain low-interest financial market have been causing falling growth rates in the island nation since 2011. The bottom was reached in 2015 for the time being. Last year saw a slight increase in economic development as a result of massive investment in the country's infrastructure. The delayed effects of current infrastructure-focused policies should continue to have a positive impact on economic development in the coming years. Nevertheless, in September 2016, the Asian Development Bank downgraded its growth forecasts for Indonesia for the year 2017 from 5.5 to 5.1 percent for the time being. With this forecast, the Asian Development Bank is well below the goals of the Jokowi government, which has targeted seven percent economic growth in 2017. This would lead to lower tax revenues

---

30) EKONID (Ed.), Indonesia, Business Potential for the Energ Utilization of Geothermal Energy Target Market Analysis 2017, www.german-energy-solutions.de

than planned and already initiated infrastructure measures would have to be postponed.[31)]

With the Master Plan to Accelerate and Strengthen the Economic Development of Indonesia (abbreviated to MP3EI) 12, the previous government under Bambang Susilo Yudhoyono set the most ambitious long-term development program in many years in 2011. By implementing the development programs defined there, Indonesia should become one of the ten leading economies by 2025. Gross domestic product is expected to rise to $ 4.5 trillion and GDP per capita up to $ 15,500. The master plan is based on three central objectives[32)]:

Expansion of value chains in industrial production and qualification of the distribution network; better access of industry to natural resources and human capital;

stimulating production efficiency and better integration of domestic markets;

Strengthening the national innovation system.

Possible strategies include a favorable policy on tariffs, taxes, import duties, labor regulations, licensing and land acquisition.

31) EKONID (Ed.), 2017, ibid.
32) EKONID (Ed.), 2017, ibid.

The MP3EI defines eight sectors that should be the focus of economic development: agriculture, mining, energy, industry, tourism, telecommunications and certain strategic regions. Specifically, 22 priority areas are defined within these eight programs.[33)]

There are 396 major infrastructure projects in MP3EI, many of which are already completed or in the implementation phase. Overall, the implementation of 1,048 projects is planned. The formation of public-private partnerships for financing is given high priority.[34)]

Energy and Renewable Energy

Indonesia's government plans to invest nearly US $ 90 billion in power generation and distribution between 2015 and 2019. She can not handle this sum alone and relies on private commitment. The first, especially state-owned enterprises, have expressed their interest in the construction of power plants. In particular, plants based on coal, gas or biodiesel are planned. In total, the electricity consumption of the archipelago in 2014 amounted to 199 terawatt hours (TWh). Production should increase to over 350 TWh by 2020 and exceed the 1,000 TWh limit after 2040. In addition to the continued strong use of fos-

33) EKONID (Ed.), 2017, ibid.
34) EKONID (Ed.), 2017, ibid.

sil fuels, the share of renewable energies in the electricity mix should also be increased. The alternative generation capacity is expected to double between 2014 and 2019. At the end of 2014, renewable energies with a total capacity of almost 11,000 MW were installed. Of this, 70% was generated by hydropower. The rest shared geothermal and biomass. In the meantime, wind and solar energy played practically no role whatsoever. The government is particularly keen to promote geothermal energy, as the Southeast Asian archipelago is located on a long line of volcanoes, the so-called Ring of Fire. 40% of the world's (theoretically) usable geothermal energy is in Indonesia.[35)]

Agriculture and food processing

The agricultural sector is one of the largest industries in Indonesia. In 2014, together with fisheries and forestry, it contributed about 14% to gross domestic product, according to the BPS. Here agriculture plays an important role as foreign currency. In recent decades, the oil palm has become Indonesia's most economically successful plant. Their cultivation partially displaces the classic cash crops such as coffee, tea, cocoa or sugarcane. The oil palm crops - but also tea and sugar cane - are mainly grown on large plantations. Especially invest-

---

35) German Trade & Invest (Ed.), 2016, ibid.

ors from Malaysia have built up a strong position in the palm oil business. However, in 2014 the government curtailed the involvement of foreign investors. In contrast, cocoa, coffee and many nut and spice varieties are grown almost exclusively by smaller local farmers. Most of the 27 million tonnes of palm oil produced annually is exported. Indonesia is the world's largest exporter of palm oil.[36)]

Coal and mining

In 2014, exports of mining products (excluding oil and gas) decreased 27% year-over-year to 23 billion $. But this development did not affect all sectors. In coal mining, for example, Indonesia has become a leading exporter and promoter in recent years. In 2013, national output was around 450 million tonnes. Compared to 2003, this represents an increase of five times. For 2015, however, a decline to 425 million tonnes was expected. Many mines restrict their operation in view of the low prices. Indonesian coal is known for its low sulfur content and enjoys great popularity in countries struggling with high air pollution. Structural changes are in progress in other areas: in January 2014, the government banned the export of certain unprocessed mineral ores. It wants to achieve that new molten metals are built and thus more added value remains in

---

36) German Trade & Invest (Ed.), 2016, ibid.

Germany - temporary exemptions could, however, be granted. The East Asian vehicle industry, but also other sectors, urgently depend on Indonesian supplies. They traditionally source large quantities of nickel ores and bauxite from the archipelago. Therefore, it is not surprising that this region is particularly interested in the construction of metallurgical plants.[37)]

Oil and gas

Indonesia's oil reserves are slowly coming to an end. The vast majority of sources only generate decreasing production volumes. New deposits are mainly in the east of the archipelago on the high seas. However, the offshore operation is much more expensive and time-consuming and only worthwhile with rising oil prices. This deters investors. The country has changed from being a net exporter to becoming an importer of oil and fuel, and in 2008 withdrew from the Organization of Petroleum Exporting Countries (OPEC). Since then, the gap between imports and exports has steadily increased in this sector. In 2014, imports totaled $ 40.4 billion, while exports amounted to only $ 13.2 billion. The reasons for this development: On the one hand, due to insufficient investment in new fields, the production volume has shrunk noticeably. On the other hand, the domestic gasoline and diesel consumption has risen rapidly

37) German Trade & Invest (Ed.), 2016, ibid.

through a rapid motorization and generous subsidy of fuel prices.[38)]

Infrastructure

Nationwide, roads, waterways and railways need urgent expansion in order to increase the growth rates of the economy. According to the calculation of the national planning authority from 2015 to 2019, investment needs in the area of infrastructure amount to about 440 billion US $. The sum should be raised to 50% by the public sector. Almost 20% will contribute to state enterprises. The rest should come from private investors. The first PPP projects are in the post tendering or construction phase. At the end of 2013, work on a first section of a subway line in Jakarta started. Other projects are not running so smoothly: The start of construction for a power plant complex on Java had to be postponed several times, because there were difficulties in land purchase. Almost all stalled infrastructure projects suffer from this problem.[39)]

2. Innovation system

The Dutch in Indonesia for more than 300 years of colonial rule, and build the modern education system. From the 1949,

38) German Trade & Invest (Ed.), 2016, ibid.
39) German Trade & Invest (Ed.), 2016, ibid.

Indonesia won the independence and over the Holland's colonial rule. Since independence, Indonesian education has served on the national construction and economic construction, in the elementary education, secondary education and higher education have made significant achievements.

After the Indonesian economy has entered a new phase, the Indonesian government stipulates that all public and private college freshmen must take part in the study of Panchakira and only graduate 100 hours before graduating. According to the third long-term development strategy for higher education in 1996, higher education reform must clarify these existing problems[40]:

(1) Higher education requires a diversity of models to cope with dramatic changes at home and abroad; (2) Takes education quality and interdisciplinarity as a reference for the development of higher education; (3) Improves social services through higher education reforms ability.

The core of the strategy is[41]: (1) Implementing a new management model; (2) Improving the quality of teaching and the connection between disciplines; (3) Safeguarding the fairness and equality of society. The improvement of the quality of higher education is a key part of improving the quality of education.

---

40) Zhang Dan, Research on the development of education since independence in Indonesia, Guizhou Shifan Daxue, 2017, at: www.cnki.net

41) ibid

1) The duration of higher education is 3 to 5 years, and students can graduate with full credit.

In addition, the government has also reformed the teaching plans and admission methods of higher education institutions in order to cultivate more talents to serve the new order economy. The reformed Indonesian higher education adopts a degree teaching plan and a non-degree teaching plan. The degree teaching program is divided into two phases. One is for junior college students and the other for undergraduate students. After a few years of study, the student obtains a certain degree of credit, and he has an associate degree and a bachelor's degree. The second is the postgraduate stage. After the end of the study, master' s degrees, doctoral degrees, etc. are granted after passing the dissertation' s defense.

2) The degree teaching program is mainly to train senior talents and academic research talents. After the students enter school, if they have not achieved satisfactory results in their studies or have not cultivated their career prospects, they will be granted associate degree degrees and will finish their studies ahead of schedule. Therefore, an associate degree is viewed as a checkpoint for the selection of top talent.

The non-degree teaching program is designed to allow more young students to have access to higher education and master more knowledge and skills. After entering the school, students may study for a short period of time of one or two years. They may be ten to eleven years old. After they graduate from school, they will receive a diploma and be recognized by the society so that they can find jobs easily. For higher education institutions, non-degree teaching programs are mainly designed to limit the number of university graduates. Since 1984, the Indonesian government has implemented the "new college entrance examination system." The main contents are[42]:

First, some of the top students are reviewed by officials from local representative agencies of the Ministry of Culture and Education, secondary school principals and universities. The remaining graduates took the national unified examination.

Third, candidates can choose two volunteers, the first choice for the university where they are admitted, and the second choice for the other exam district universities. Candidates can only take one test. Those with good grades can go to the ten most famous universities. If they have poor grades, they may go to other institutions of higher learning or normal schools or participate in non-degree teaching programs.

The new college entrance examination system actually divides the candidates into three categories through examinations:

---

42) ibid

The first category is excellent students, who are guaranteed to be exempt from the test. The second type is students with moderate academic performance. They participate in the National Unified Examination and are admitted to the National University Open University. The third type of students have poor academic performance or intelligence, enter the labor market, or participate in adult higher education and receive diplomas.[43)]

The reform of the new college entrance examination system has led to an increase in the number of Indonesian college graduates participating in the college entrance examination, and the number of admissions has also shown an upward trend with the reform of the college entrance examination system. More and more students have thus entered the universities of higher education, and are also national Economic construction has delivered more talents.

In addition, the Indonesian Ministry of Culture and Education decided in 1985 that no new colleges and universities would be added in the next few years, but that they would control the quality of institutions of higher learning on an established basis. At the same time, private institutions of higher learning are gradually reorganized. If they do not meet the teaching

43) ibid

quality and teaching requirements, they will be disqualified or merged. Moreover, in order to improve the quality of college students, the Indonesian government began a nationwide graduation exam from the fourth five-year plan and insisted on phasing out college students who had not progressed academically.[44]

After entering the 1990s, Indonesia's private universities, which have undergone rectification, thrived and the number of schools far exceeded that of national universities. Since the National University is mostly a science and engineering university, it undertakes science and engineering education, and it trains high-level professionals, so the graduation rate of students is strictly controlled. In addition, Indonesian universities also focus on social services.

Students are required not only to complete their studies but also to assume certain social responsibilities. The school will regularly organize students to go to the countryside for volunteer services and help. Religious universities often go to religious places to teach teachings.

From the perspective of professional selection, the number of people choosing engineering and economic majors is also increasing year by year. The choice of students for majors can al-

44) ibid

so reflect the society's demand for engineering and economic talents. Before the Asian financial crisis in 1997, higher education in Indonesia has been growing rapidly. According to the "National Report of Indonesia" published by London, England, from 1995 to 1996, "Indonesia has 49 state universities and 950 private institutions of higher learning. "[45]

Second, the country is divided into three test areas, the first test area includes Sumatra, Jakarta, West Java area; the second test area includes Yogyakarta, Central Java, and Kalimantan areas; the third test area includes East Java, Sulawesi, Iri An area. Candidates can go to the nearby to apply for a test.[46]

45) ibid
46) ibid

Chapter 5 Innovation System in Myanmar

I. Country Profile and Historical Characteristics

Burma/Myanmar, one of the world's least developed countries, with a population of around 50 million, borders Thailand, Laos, China, India and Bangladesh. Since gaining independence in 1948, civil strife has been almost uninterrupted, with government forces battling communist insurgents, ethnic minority rebels and militants of drug traffickers. Myanmar's capital has been Naypyidaw since 2005. The largest city in the country and the economic center is Yangon with 5.4 million inhabitants. The official language is Burmese, besides languages of numerous ethnic minorities are common. Business language of the former British colony is English. Myanmar is characterized by scenic and climatic diversity, from the coastal region on the Bay of Bengal over the dry zone in the country center to the Himalayan foothills in the north. Predominant is a subtropical climate with peak temperatures of up to 40 ℃. The rainy season extends from June to October.

II. Political Development

According to current democratic theories, the right to freedom of expression, association and assembly is a must, so that citizens can form independent opinions and express them publicly. Thus, these liberties are a necessary condition for meaningful elections. Freedom rights also allow for the emergence of an active civil society that articulates collective demands on the state. Even in "top-down" regime change (as one can assume in Myanmar, as the military (Tatmadaw) initiated the reforms in 2011 on its own and continues to have veto power in many areas), civil society actors can put pressure on further reforms in the direction of Increase democracy and therefore be a key success factor for democratization. In addition, civil liberties are central to the rule of law. The rule of law subjects all actions of citizens and of the state to written down law, which in turn is subject to the premise of universal human rights, which include fundamental liberties. If Myanmar has actually moved towards democracy, then at least since 2011, one must be able to recognize a positive development of practiced liberties.[1)]

1) Andy Buschmann, Protest und Demokratisierung in Myanmar: Erste Erkenntnisse aus dem „Myanmar Protest Event Dataset " [Protest and Democratization in Myanmar: First Insights from the „Myanmar Protest Event Dataset "], in: Asiatische Studien - Études Asiatiques · February 2018

Burma / Myanmar, which has been independent since 1948, has been governed since 1962 by a military dictatorship, with the exception of the period 1974-1988, when there was a one-party system. From the outside, the government system seems to be centralized. In fact, however, it is highly fragmented and the decision-making processes and ways of government action are obscure. Above all, the different ethnic groups of Burma demand the granting of real autonomy for their homelands and a clear say in matters affecting the whole country. Since the coup d'état of 1988, military leaders have signed 17 cease-fire agreements with ethnic minority armed groups, granting them autonomy to varying degrees and, in some cases, the right to retain their own armed forces. In many areas for which a truce has been concluded, there is only an unstable truce. In particular, the KNU (Karen National Union) and the SSA (Shan State Army) continue to offer armed resistance to the military, but both are increasingly losing influence over previously "liberated" areas.[2)]

After decades of isolation, Myanmar is now in a phase of social, economic and political change. With the election of ex-General Thein Sein as President in February 2011, far-reaching reforms were launched. Among other things, these reforms

---

2) Andy Buschmann, 2018, ibid.

allowed the election victory of Aung San Suu Kyi and her party, the National League for Democracy (NLD), in November 2015. For this reason, many observers see Myanmar in a political transition, at best, in the direction of democracy since 2011 at the latest. However, it is not just elections and parliaments that make for a representative democracy, as many (western) governments in Myanmar wish , this includes. Freedom rights and civic engagement are also substantial components of democracy. So the question is, how have these dimensions changed in Myanmar since 2011?[3)]

After gaining independence from Great Britain in 1948, the country was initially led by a fragile civilian government before it came to a military coup in March 1962. As a result, the armed forces, called Tatmadaw, took control and ruled the country under the rule of army chief Ne Win until the late 1980s in the style of a military dictatorship. Myanmar pursued a policy of self-isolation and neutralism during this period. In 1988, a pro-democracy uprising was violently crushed by the regime. Ne Win was deposed by a generation of younger officers who came to power as a collective. On the basis of a new state council for the restoration of law and order (1997 re-

3) Andy Buschmann, 2018, ibid.

named State Council for Peace and Development) established the Tatmadaw a form of military rule.[4)]

The developments observable since 2008 in Myanmar give rise to two different conclusions. On the one hand, it is true that a genuine reform process can be identified, which aims at transferring government responsibility to civilian actors. On the other hand, the military consolidates their position of power in the state at the same time. In 2008, for example, a new constitution was passed, which was to form the basis for democratization and became the basis for the parliamentary elections of November 2010. However, 25% of all parliamentary seats are reserved for the armed forces in this constitution. Also, various provisions protect the institutional privileges of the military. In addition, the constitution gives the army chief the right to appoint defense, interior and border control ministers. In turn, constitutional amendments require a three-quarters majority in parliament.[5)]

For its part, the 2010 parliamentary elections were criticized internationally as neither free nor fair, as various opposition figures such as Nobel Peace Prize laureate Aung San Suu Kyi

---

4) CSS Analysis on Security Policy, Myanmar: Political Reforms and Military Preservation, No. 115, June 2012

5) CSS Analysis on Security Policy, Myanmar: Political Reforms and Military Preservation, No. 115, June 2012

were not allowed to attend and the Union Solidarity and Development Party (USDP) backed by the military junta secured 76.5% of the vote could. As a result, however, the regime made remarkable efforts to involve NLD leader Suu Kyi more closely, thereby gaining international legitimacy. Under the leadership of President Thein Sein, a moderate former general elected by the People's Assembly in February 2011, the increasingly civilian government has since made large concessions to the opposition leader. These include the removal of house arrest and a constitutional amendment that allows her to vote as a candidate. Several hundred political prisoners have also been released.[6)]

The term of office of the new democratically elected government in Myanmar begins with a double bang: Aung San Suu Kyi's ascent to the Foreign Minister and "State Councilor" has given the long-time opposition leader what the military wanted to do for over 25 years. Since April 6, 2016 Suu Kyi de facto the government business. Htin Kyaw, president of the National League for Democracy (NLD), is a long-time party member and devoted supporter of Suu Kyi, the head of state on paper.[7)]

6) CSS Analysis on Security Policy, Myanmar: Political Reforms and Military Preservation, No. 115, June 2012

7) Konstantin Baerwaldt, 2016, Daring More Democracy in Myanmar Challenges for the Government under Aung San Suu Kyi, International Policy Analysis, Friedrich Ebert Foundation

The young, somewhat libertarian democracy, in which liberal civil rights have increasingly been admitted and tolerated by the regime in recent years, is threatened not only by the continuing strong role of the military: the continuing civil wars, the sometimes systematic exclusion of ethnic and religious minorities The state and Buddhist majority society as well as a blatant prosperity gap all threaten the foundations of a democracy based on social balance and socio-economic participation.[8)]

For Myanmar to master the transformation from an electoral to a social rights-fulfilling democracy in the medium and long term, satisfying the expectations of some 52 million citizens for a better life, three basic conditions must be met[9)]:

1) Democratic control of the military and redefinition of the relationship between state and military;

2) peace between the ethnic groups and re-adjustment of the relationship between state and society;

3) Fundamental reform of the political economy with noticeable redistributive effects in favor of the army of millions of the poor.

---

8) Konstantin Baerwaldt, 2016, ibid.
9) Konstantin Baerwaldt, 2016, ibid.

The most obvious challenge to the young democratic entity is the continuing dominance of the military and the associated weakness of democratic control. Despite - or perhaps because - the first-time government takeover by the NLD and a devastating deselection of the previous military government under President Thein Sein, the generals have underpinned their claim to power in recent weeks and want to continue to have a say in the fate of the country.[10)]

The mistrust between NLD and Tatmadaw is abysmal. After Suu Kyi was still on reconciliation with the military until the elections in November 2015, she went on the offensive following the overwhelming victory of her NLD. Systematically she has developed her own power base.

For the military, the unstoppable rise of their adversary with the creation of the post of State Councilor and the replacement of the Constitutional Tribunal has not yet ended. The power-spoiled army had to watch as the NLD, coming from the 25-year fundamentalist opposition, systematically expanded its power base since forming a government. Contrary to the demands of the general government, President Htin Kyaw made use of his constitutional right to fill all fourteen prime ministers in the countries and regions with NLD candidates. Due to the

10) Konstantin Baerwaldt, 2016, ibid.

ongoing civil wars in the Shan state and the Kachin state on the border with China and a massive troop presence of the Tatmadaw in these areas, the military had demanded to nominate the heads of state themselves. Since national security was also endangered by the Muslim Rohingyas in the Rakhine state, the generals also wanted to provide the local Chief Minister. In Yangon, the country's economic boom region, a retainer should be installed to maintain control over economic developments. However, the NLD refused the request of the army.[11)]

Despite the open exchange between the NLD and the military, the armed forces seem to have come to terms with the rapid growth of their civil counterparts. Because still the Tatmadaw is firmly anchored in the state apparatus. The fact that the army will guide the Myanmar state in the future, both formally and realistically, will be ensured by constitutional precautions, its special financial privileges and the decades-long penetration of the military-state complex by officers and soldiers. The military remains an institution independent of the political apparatus. Three influential ministers in the cabinet of NLD President Htin Kyaw are in the direct command chain of the Commander-in-Chief. The Ministry of the Interior, the Ministry of Defense and the Ministry of Border Security are run

11) Konstantin Baerwaldt, 2016, ibid.

by generals who are not responsible to the government or the elected representatives of the people.[12]

The General Administrative Department (GAD), a subordinate agency of the Ministry of the Interior and the backbone of the public administration, continues to rule after the change of government with centralized violence in all around 64,000 villages and municipalities in the country. The reform years 2011-2016 passed almost without a trace at the authority. The GAD is responsible for a variety of governmental tasks, such as: As the tax collection, the regulation of land issues or the issue of licenses. For many citizens outside the cities, the GAD is what people most likely perceive as "state" in their everyday lives.[13]

Even under Thein Sein, several dozen ex-officers were sent to leadership positions to implement the Ministry of Interior policy at the local level. The NLD legal adviser, Ko Ni, points out that the NLD government will not be able to enforce any policy against this powerful authority without the consent of the military.[14]

After the bloody suppression of the popular uprising of 1988 and the subsequent seizure of power, the military government planned to exercise its duties only temporarily. With the draft-

12) Konstantin Baerwaldt, 2016, ibid.

13) Konstantin Baerwaldt, 2016, ibid.

14) Konstantin Baerwaldt, 2016, ibid.

ing of the 2008 constitution, it created the conditions for a transfer of power, ordered from its perspective, to a civilian government and partial withdrawal. Without taking these motives into consideration, it would not be possible to explain why the military in fact pushed the process of opening and modernization and allowed itself to be "deselected" by free elections.[15)]

But it is also beyond dispute that the Tatmadaw will show no willingness to compromise on questions of national security and state identity - of course stretchable constructs that were regularly used in the past for interfering with educational, health, cultural and social policies. The purpose of the Myanmar military goes far beyond the "classical" role of armed forces as guarantors of security. Since the founding of Myanmar, the function of the military as a "guardian of the nation" has been closely linked to the development of the state. According to its self-conception, the Tatmadaw is the only functioning institution of the country, which is able to unite the multi-ethnic state and to protect the fragile state structure from politicians who are only concerned about their particular interests. Whether in coping with the invasion of the Kuomintang in the 1950s, repelling ethnic rebel groups in the first two decades after the founding of the state, or suppressing

15) Konstantin Baerwaldt, 2016, ibid.

the popular uprising of 1988, the military class has always failed in times of national emergency.[16)]

In order to prevent a repetition of these dangers for all eternity, the military has written a special clause in the constitution: As ultima ratio, the commander-in-chief, or rather the national security council dominated by him, has the right to act in times of crisis. Civilians are a minority in the eleven-member Security Council. The NLD can only send five representatives to the panel. In addition to Foreign Minister Suu Kyi, the president and the vice-president are entitled to vote as well as the two speakers of parliament. The remaining six positions are occupied by the military.[17)]

Out of military self-perception, the conflict with the new government goes far beyond the hostility of Suu Kyi and her party. No matter which civilians are at the head of the state. For the Tatmadaw, the constitution is the ruling social contract for a polity designed for eternity that can not be denounced by anyone. Commander-in-Chief Min Aung Hlaing, in his speech to the National Day of the Armed Forces, underlined that the

---

16) Andy Buschmann, Myanmar Protest and Democratization: First Findings from the Myanmar Protest Event Dataset [Myanmar Protest and Democratization: First Insights from the Myanmar Protest Event Dataset], Asian Studies - Études Asiatiques, February 2018

17) Andy Buschmann, 2018, ibid.

army would support "current developments and changes" within the given system, but warned that there were no deviations from the fulfillment of the constitutional definition defined by the military Would allow the state to do so - "the unresolvability of the Union, the indivisibility of national solidarity, the maintenance of sovereignty". This shows the explosiveness of current developments.[18)]

While the Tatmadaw stands for the preservation of the existing, Suu Kyi and her party from the perspective of the military on the foundations of the nation shake. The situation is even more unstable because even the approximately twenty armed groups of ethnic minorities reject the current constitution. For different reasons Suu Kyi and ethnic minorities still find state and nation building an unfinished project. They never recognized the state treaty imposed by the military. With the replacement of the Ancien regime by Suu Kyi and the NLD, the debate over the legitimacy and distribution of state power gains a whole new dynamic and dimension that threatens to divide the identity of the military.[19)]

A true horror scenario for the military is therefore the invitation of the Council of State to all hostile civil war parties for

---

18) Andy Buschmann, 2018, ibid.
19) Andy Buschmann, 2018, ibid.

a national peace conference. As unrealistic as the chances of success are, the attempt underscores the historical ambitions of the government. Suu Kyi and her supporters want to achieve what all previous governments have failed for over sixty years: the negotiation of a new state and social contract that could redistribute the structural power weights. The historical symbolism of such a conference should not be underestimated. With her offer Suu Kyi deftly staged as a leader and heir of her father still revered as a hero in Myanmar today. General and founder Aung San had signed an agreement in 1947 at the post-conference "Panglong Conference" with the leaders of various ethnic groups in the East and North on their autonomy.[20]

But even before it could be implemented, Myanmar's acclaimed freedom fighter was murdered. Afterwards, Myanmar, which had just become independent from Great Britain, sank into numerous civil wars that have not ended or flared up again in some parts of the country to this day. About 40 percent of the Myanmar population belongs to about 20 ethnic groups. Due to the decades of civil wars, the central state was unable to assert its claim to sovereignty in all parts of the country. In some cases, ethnic minority armed groups have built parallel state structures and are responsible for providing education, health and public security.[21]

20) Andy Buschmann, 2018, ibid.

With the military claiming sole authority over issues of internal and external security, Suu Kyi and its NLD ministers can not make any concessions to rebel groups that are not sanctioned by the military. Under these circumstances, it remains questionable what negotiation offers the NLD government will make to the ethnic groups at the upcoming conference. A political representative of a group of Shan rightly pointed out that all negotiating results would be worthless if they were not subsequently implemented by the military.[22]

Even during the military-friendly term of President and ex-General Thein Sein, the military had repeatedly resisted government orders and independently created political facts through its warfare. The latest military offensive in the Rakhine state has certainly not been decided upon in consultation with President Htin Kyaw or Suu Kyi. The purely technical ceasefire talks, the hardliners among the rebel groups will not get involved - they want political concessions. The failed negotiations of the last three years have already shown that.[23]

Given the complexity and fundamental differences in interests, Suu Kyi and the government can not count on overcoming decades of mistrust between the military and minority

---

21) Andy Buschmann, 2018, ibid.

22) Konstantin Baerwaldt, 2016, ibid.

23) Konstantin Baerwaldt, 2016, ibid.

groups with pure conference diplomacy. The symbolism is important and correct, but a national meeting of the conflicting parties will not be enough.

As if the challenges for the young democracy, with the continuing military dominance and the ongoing civil wars, are not enough, without democracy, the promotion of emancipative and creative social forces, and pluralism, democracy will not be able to gain ground in Myanmar in the medium term. Ironically, behind this challenge - the readjustment of the relationship between the state and society - are in the NLD government and her celebrated as a "democracy icon" Suu Kyi big question marks. Real politicians and technocrats may dismiss democratic participation and inclusion as subordinate development goals, but if the numerous multi-ethnic and multi-religious groups in Myanmar are not better integrated into state and society, the "democratic project" will remain an authoritarian-managed elite project.[24)]

The systematic exclusion and deprivation of rights of the ethnic group of the approximately 1.1 million Muslim Rohingya is the best-known example of the exclusionary policy of the Myanmar state practiced for decades. The NLD, which is now part of the new state elite, has so far shown no signs of perse-

24) Konstantin Baerwaldt, 2016, ibid.

cution in governmental responsibility. The pressure of the majority Buddhist population, especially from the Rakhine state, where the vast majority of Rohingyas live, is too great. A retired Myanmar diplomat in a confidential conversation expressed his concern that any concession from Suu Kyi to the Rohingyas could lead to the premature end of their government, so heated is the public mood. Therefore, the NLD government continues the policy of discrimination.[25)]

The NLD does not seem willing to oppose the Buddhist popular anger against the Muslims at present. Popular anti-Muslim and misogynist laws, which were enforced by the previous government against the opposition of dozens of human rights groups, should not be reformed for the time being. Unlike promised in the election campaign, Suu Kyi does not have a "government of national unity" that does justice to the country's social diversity.[26)]

The Burmese-Buddhist notion of the "great chosen one" knows best what is good for their people. But this does not have to be included in decision-making and the state power apparatus. This explains why the Buddhist majority society stoically took note that Suu Kyi initially wanted to take over four

25) Konstantin Baerwaldt, 2016, ibid.
26) Konstantin Baerwaldt, 2016, ibid.

ministerial offices at once. Their demand to always be above the president is safe for a large part of the population. Representatives of ethnic minority groups, such as For example, Shan politician Ye Htun warned that a "uncontrolled" parliament and civil society Suu Kyi could easily fall into the role of a "dictatorial leader".[27)]

The free speech of NLD Members in Parliament is not allowed. All debates must be approved in advance by a party committee chaired by Suu Kyi. Also at events organized by trade unions and civil society organizations NLD politicians are not allowed to attend without being asked. The burgeoning civil society will not be discouraged by the decades-long cultivation of the leadership culture - not even under an NLD-led government. The emancipatory awareness of the thousands of displaced persons, the approximately 80,000 organized workers, the student associations, the journalists journalists, the ethnically based human rights organizations and the intellectuals has grown too much in the past five years. Already under the presidency of Thein Sein, these groups have learned that they can effectively build pressure on the political elite outside of formal decision-making. A prominent example is the temporary freezing of the Myitsone Dam on the Irrawaddy River. Thousands of people had protested together with civil society groups from

27) Konstantin Baerwaldt, 2016, ibid.

around the country against the billion-dollar construction project. Massive resistance is also directed against other infrastructure projects in the country, which are usually planned and built without the participation of the citizens concerned.[28)]

Already after one and a half months NLD regency now turn the first frustrated from the party. But they continue to fight for their cause: whether the trade unionists are in favor of fair wages, the students for an emancipative education policy, the farmers for the right to self-determined cultivation, the journalists for free access to information or the rural population against the construction of Industrial parks on their land. The local politicians of the NLD and the party base feel the conflicts on the ground; they are the first addressees of the protest. And they worry about the future of the party. Because the leadership is mainly concerned with the securing of power and the repression of the military.[29)]

However, if the new leadership does not deliver on its auspicious promises of rule of law, democratic participation and economic justice, then NLD-led democracy will be challenged much more quickly than it has to fight for the replacement of military rule.[30)]

---

28) Konstantin Baerwaldt, 2016, ibid.
29) Konstantin Baerwaldt, 2016, ibid.
30) Konstantin Baerwaldt, 2016, ibid.

In this regard, one can observe civil society organization in the country. In Myanmar, there is now a very visible diversity in civil society actors - especially in the fields of education, health and environmental protection, community development and gender. The country's ethnic and cultural diversity is reflected in the diversity of civil society actors in the country, many of whom have an ethnic or religious background.[31)]

The most common forms of civil society organization are Local Non-Governmental Organizations (LNGOs), Community-Based Organizations (CBOs), and denominational, student, trade union, and youth associations. The LNGOs directory in Myanmar, published annually by the Local Resource Center (LRC), lists as many as 118 local non-governmental organizations (NGOs) in 2012, which are expected to grow in the coming years.[32)]

Faith-oriented organizations and associations (especially Buddhist, Islamic, Christian and Hindu) are not only historically but also up-to-date, characteristic of the country and provide an important basis for people's lives. A focus of many local organizations is the charity sector with the Focus on social welfare of communities and affected populations. In addition to commun-

31) Christina Grein, New Freedoms, New Protests, Civil Society Voices and Action in: Departure in Myanmar, Koeln, 2013

32) Christina Grein, 2013, ibid.

ity capacity building, advocacy work at both local and national level is also playing an increasingly important role. After several decades of civil war, militarization and state repression, spaces have once again opened up for social and political organization. Even though the degree of global networking is still manageable, regional networks have become a driving force for civil society action.[33]

Scopes and barriers Some LNGOs have now, to a limited extent, been able to work together with the government on important political issues concerning foreign investment, the environment and land rights, and to provide analyzes and policy recommendations. Further existing restrictions are the current registration law and the dominance of important state institutions.[34]

One of the main players in the field of investment remains state-controlled, the Myanmar Investment Commission (MIC), located under the Ministry of National Planning and Economic Development and responsible for examining domestic investment. Reform proposals for the Investment Act in 2012 include the proposal to transform the Commission into an independent body, thus increasing the transparency of the award-

33) Christina Grein, 2013, ibid.
34) Christina Grein, 2013, ibid.

ing of investment licenses. However, key positions continue to be filled by senior state representatives. Civil society groups call for inclusion in political / economic decision-making processes, not only in areas such as democratization and human rights, but especially in business and development.[35)]

Myanmar has taken the biggest hurdle on the way to democracy for the time being: Aung San Suu Kyi and the National League for Democracy (NLD) led by her could form a government that for the first time in more than 50 years represented the electoral will of a large majority of the people. The old military government peacefully made room for the civilians.

The young democracy in Myanmar remains threatened by three simultaneous challenges: the institutionalized veto power of the military in a war-torn country, the repressive relationship between the state and society, and the massive gaps in prosperity. These mortgages weigh heavily on the democratically elected government under Quasi-Prime Minister Aung San Suu Kyi. Addressing these issues is a multi-generation task. Without active civic participation, democratic development will remain an authoritarian managed elite project.

The army fears that the civil-run government and ethnic minority armed groups could question the nation's foundations at

35) Christina Grein, 2013, ibid.

the upcoming "Panglong Conference for the 21st Century." For the military, the nation-building process is completed with the 2008 State Treaty. Political and economic reforms are tolerated only within the framework of the existing order. The prerequisite for massive poverty reduction and economic modernization is a strong state of development.[36)]

III. Economic Transformation and Innovation Systemar

1. Economic Transformation

Myanmar, formerly Burma, is one of the largest countries in Southeast Asia with an area of over 676,000 km^2 . The country has been at the center of international attention since the political opening in 2011. Burma / Myanmar is a poor country despite its rich natural resources. Corruption, a lack of knowledge about economic interactions and international isolation have led to economic stagnation despite short-lived efforts to liberalize the economy in the late 1980s. Per capita GDP in 2003 was around 179 $. Industrialization is still in its infancy and agriculture, which accounts for nearly 60% of the country's GDP, continues to play a key role. As a consequence of the government's policy of rejuvenating the economy between 1989

36) Konstantin Baerwaldt, 2016, ibid.

and 1999 after three decades of centrally planned economy, Burma / Myanmar today has a mixed economy. Private sector activity has increased, focusing mainly on agriculture, light industry and transport. However, the private sector is dominated by a small number of entrepreneurs enjoying the trust of the military government.[37)]

There is also an extensive illegal economy centered around the smuggling of drugs6, diamonds and tropical wood. The proceeds of this illicit trade benefit armed groups - including both ethnic minorities who have signed ceasefire agreements and those that are not - but also the Burmese / Myanmar military, which makes it difficult to tackle this problem which nourishes the conflict as well as leads to a long-term unsustainable exploitation of resources. Moreover, the profits from this illegal trade do not "leak" into the population and do not contribute to poverty eradication or livelihoods.[38)]

Corruption is part of the system in politics and the economy. The military government deliberately pursues a policy of nepotism and grants privileges such as licenses for car imports or telephone operators, beneficiary companies and family

37) Strategiepapier der EG fuer Birma/Myanmar 2007-2013, http://edz.bib.uni-mannheim.de/daten/edz-ma/gdex/07/07_23_de.pdf

38) Strategiepapier der EG fuer Birma/Myanmar 2007-2013, http://edz.bib.uni-mannheim.de/daten/edz-ma/gdex/07/07_23_de.pdf

members. The uncertain legal framework leads to pure profit-making at all levels of economic life. To a lesser extent, corruption is also part of a public sector workers' coping strategy that does not receive adequate salaries. Public spending in Burma / Myanmar is one of the lowest in the world (around 4% of GDP). Nevertheless, spending exceeds revenue, causing a budget deficit. The government's austerity measures make public investment in basic humanitarian and social infrastructures even more difficult, despite the huge demand.[39)]

Traditionally, Myanmar's economic structure is shaped by agriculture. Overall, the agricultural sector contributes 32% to gross domestic product and 20% to export revenues, according to the OECD. However, the industry, with its comparatively low wages, currently employs around 70% of the population. The agricultural sector offers great potential for expansion and diversification, but requires some structural and technological modernization. Because most farms are small farms at subsistence level.

To ensure more dynamic development, modern farm technologies and agro-cultural research must be promoted. In addition, the expertise on modern cultivation methods and yield in-

---

39) Strategiepapier der EG fuer Birma/Myanmar 2007-2013, http://edz.bib.uni-mannheim.de/daten/edz-ma/gdex/07/07_23_de.pdf

creases is missing. Therefore, German companies also have business opportunities with regard to machinery, equipment, agricultural chemistry and technical know-how. With its new strategic plan, the government wants to rejoin old record crops in rice production.[40)]

The food and beverage industry dominates with about two-thirds of the manufacturing sector. Of a total of 38,683 manufacturing companies, 25,965 are in the food sector. Most processors use traditional production methods. Thus, an upgrade of existing facilities is required to fully exploit growth potential. Edible oils, fruit juices, milk (pasteurized, condensed, vaporized), yoghurt and dehydrated vegetables and various snack foodstuffs for export are considered interesting. The food and beverage sector offers great potential for foreign direct investment. Major corporations around the world have already been attracted - including Coca-Cola, PepsiCo, Nestle, Unilever, Carlsberg, Heineken, Mitsubishi or Charoen Pokphand Foods and Tropical Premier Foods. Represented by dominant companies, Thailand is the largest investor in this area. For example, Charoen Pokphand Foods plans to invest over US $ 550 million with a focus on corn and rice farms, corn seeds, rice mills and

40) German Association for International Cooperation (GIZ) GmbH (Ed.), Myanmar, New Markets - New Opportunities, A Guide for German Entrepreneurs, 2015

meat processing plants. In particular, the beverage branch is experiencing strong investment activity. Coca-Cola is investing $ 300 million in a bottling plant and distribution system. In addition, PepsiCo launched the Pepsi-Cola, 7-Up and Mirinda brands and is considering investing in agriculture. In the beer industry there are new breweries from Carlsberg and Heineken.[41)]

Myanmar's garment industry is dynamically developing into a driving industry in the country's development. The government's industrial policy concept places a priority on the clothing industry. So it is to connect to their old heyday before the beginning of US economic sanctions in 2003. Taking into account all small and micro enterprises, the employment of the entire textile and clothing industry is estimated at around 250,000 people and would have almost tripled in just five years.

Regionally, the industry focuses on the industrial zones in the Greater Yangon, which is also due to the proximity to the port infrastructure and the associated logistics advantages. But other locations are also planned, for example in the Ayeyarwady

41) German Association for International Cooperation (GIZ) GmbH (Ed.), Myanmar, New Markets - New Opportunities, A Guide for German Entrepreneurs, 2015

region. A new cluster is also emerging in the Thilawa Special Economic Zone. Here, the Hong Kong Apparel Society secured 200 acres of the terrain. The market entry of major customers such as GAP or Marks & Spencer is likely to drive the industry forward. The first order samples are also produced by Swedish outfitter Hennes & Mauritz (H & M). The Myanmar Garment Manufacturers Association (MGMA) forecasts that its industry will accumulate approximately $ 1.5 billion in foreign direct investment (FDI) accumulated by 2015. Similarly, the garment industry also makes the largest contribution to the manufacturing sector in export statistics.[42)]

Electricity infrastructure with several power failures per day causes a significant cost burden for manufacturing companies. The local skills shortage results in a fragmented value chain. Thus, the industry is technologically limited to cutting, craft sewing and packaging (CMP - cutting, making, packaging), while the greater part of value added is achieved in neighboring countries. Responsible for the professional qualification is the Myanmar Garment Human Resource Development Center. These training standards are to be gradually adapted to the higher quality standards of the new foreign investors. In the

42) German Association for International Cooperation (GIZ) GmbH (Ed.), Myanmar, New Markets - New Opportunities, A Guide for German Entrepreneurs, 2015

course of its development, Myanmar's textile industry could open up interesting potential - also for German machine and plant manufacturers and textile companies. The main platform for establishing business relationships is the Myanmar International Textile and Garment Industry Exhibition in Yangon.[43)]

Whether the economic development in Myanmar is an indispensable prerequisite for the further democratization of the country, is controversial in development research with regard to comparable countries. Evidence for a causal link between democracy and development is difficult and contextual.

It is undeniable, however, that citizens will question the merits of a formal democratic system of rule if the majority of the people in Myanmar remain poor and the extreme wealth of the rich country remains concentrated on a small elite. To put it bluntly, the raging anti-Islamic mob in Rakhine State is so easy to mobilize because the region is one of the poorest in underdeveloped countries. More than 13 million women, men and children suffer from extreme poverty throughout Myanmar, according to the United Nations - which is about one quarter of the total population, and the World Bank sees even worse

43) German Association for International Cooperation (GIZ), 2015, ibid.

grievances. Especially in the remote border and conflict regions of ethnic minorities, bitter poverty still prevails.[44]

No Trickle-Down Despite Growth: The Model Remains the Old Although the country has begun a rapid economic catch-up process with the biggest growth gains in Asia in the past five years, the trickle-down effect hoped for by the Thein Sein government is during the reform years failed to materialize. The life situation of the rural population has not measurably improved. For the past five years, Myanmar has been persistently sharing the lowest rankings in Asia with Afghanistan, Pakistan and Nepal in the Human Development Index.[45]

Myanmar has been one of the Least Developed Countries since 1988. The NLD's economic program, which is little known to the public, cites the underfunding of the public budget, state mismanagement, corruption and the violation of existing laws as the main reasons for the misery. As short as the brief inventory is, it trivializes the structural deficits of the system: 50 years of military rule have left a "free market economy" constituted according to the 2008 constitution, in which exclusive patron-client networks derive profits from an extractivist pension economy and thus maintain widespread economic

44) German Association for International Cooperation (GIZ), 2015, ibid.
45) German Association for International Cooperation (GIZ), 2015, ibid.

empires. The greatest profits are made by Myanmar's plutocrats in sectors of the economy in which a nepotistic proximity to the state or military apparatus is the decisive business foundation. In almost all industries listed in The Economist's Crony-Capitalism Index, entrepreneurs also known as Cronies have their foothold: Oil, Gas, Gems, Wood, Armor, Air and Sea Ports, Construction and Infrastructure, Banks.[46)]

As a result of the reforms initiated in 2011/12, their monopoly power has increased even further. The influx of direct investment, which was more than 2,800 per cent above the 2009/10 investment in the past fiscal year, flows primarily through the channels of the plutocrats and their pupils. Around 40 percent of foreign direct investment went into the opaque commodities sector, where military and state-owned companies and pro-business people share the lucrative profits.

Since Myanmar owns one of the largest shadow economies in the world, many of the revenue is not officially recorded. Estimates suggest that about 50 percent of all profits are generated outside the formal economy. The NGO Global Witness estimated in 2014 that in the jade business alone around 28 billion US dollars were generated by the state and society.

46) German Association for International Cooperation (GIZ), 2015, ibid.

Officially, sector 12 was "only" $ 3 billion. Beneficiaries are family members of ex-commander-in-chief and dictator Than Shwe, former generals, officers, ministers and internationally sought criminals.[47)]

The state and society each year lose vast sums of potential revenue from taxes and duties that are urgently needed to finance the community. With a public budget of an estimated $ 17 billion for fiscal year 2016/17, the NLD can not make a state. Without well-funded international support, the government in many regions of the country will not even be able to provide minimum survival services for medical care and food security. Although government revenue almost doubled between 2009 and 2014 between 2009 and 2014 due to reforms and one-time license sales, Myanmar still has one of the smallest national budgets in Asia, accounting for 11 percent of GD P.[48)]

Regime change or not: According to the World Bank, nearly a third of spending has gone to the military over the past five years - more than health and education. The fact that the NLD does not make any explicit reference to the military and profiteers of the system of raw material looting in its program says

47) German Association for International Cooperation (GIZ), 2015, ibid.
48) German Association for International Cooperation (GIZ), 2015, ibid.

a lot about the actual balance of power. For the time being, the government will refrain from budget cuts for the Tatmadaw, so as not to jeopardize the political transformation. Therefore, the government needs extra money if it wants to measurably reduce poverty and make urgently needed investments in ailing public infrastructure and the non-competitive agricultural sector. Increased revenues are to be achieved through a more efficient tax system and a more consistent collection and taxation of revenues in the extractive sector.[49)]

Although the tax rates for workers and white-collar workers should remain at a comparatively low level, the tax collection should be improved. With national debt at around 47 percent of GDP in 2013/14, the NLD aims to balance revenue and expenditure. A public debt ceiling of no more than five percent per year is intended to remedy this situation. The merging and downsizing of the ministries from 36 to 21 has already been sold as an austerity measure. A fiscal federal system should ensure that the 14 regions and countries receive more attention than before from the centralized state budget. All in all, the NLD's financial and budgetary ideas follow the recommendations of the Asian Development Bank (ADB), the World Bank and the International Monetary Fund (IMF).[50)]

---

49) German Association for International Cooperation (GIZ), 2015, ibid.
50) German Association for International Cooperation (GIZ), 2015, ibid.

The "slender state" will not judge it. As plausible as the program points sound at first, they can hardly believe that this could achieve a "transformational turn" proclaimed by the NLD. Far-reaching ideas such as the creation of a sovereign wealth fund from oil, gas and other resource revenues, which was initially discussed within the party, were no longer included in the economic program.

In view of the drastic underfunding of the public budget, the NLD demand for a "lean state" is hardly comprehensible. Although government spending has risen faster than revenue over the past three years, Myanmar needs a long-term development plan that can only be financed through significantly higher spending on public infrastructure, finance, education, health and social protection. The 2013 Thein Sein strategy is similar to the NLD's plans: increased transparency in the commodity sector, combating corruption, increased tax revenues, more spending on education and social policies, people-centered development, poverty reduction and decentralization of finances.[51)]

The tasks are clear, but how can they be implemented? The challenge for Myanmar's economic transformation is less about what needs to be done than how it should be implemented. In

51) German Association for International Cooperation (GIZ), 2015, ibid.

theory, the NLD's economic program points in the right direction in the medium and long term. Economic and social development can only be achieved through the modernization of agriculture and the creation of a productive manufacturing industry. In the short and medium term, the NLD has set itself the goal of reforming ailing agriculture as the country's most important economic sector. More than one third of the gross national product is generated in the agricultural sector and around 70 percent of the Myanmar live on the production and distribution of agricultural products. Ironically in this key sector urgently needed reforms have been missing.

As late as the 1960s, Myanmar was the leading rice export nation, the "rice bowl of Asia," before the military-socialist regime of Ne Win brought the prosperous sector to a standstill through planned and quota regulations. To date, Myanmar has not recovered from this, and performs poorly in terms of both production volume and exports compared to Cambodia, Vietnam or Thailand. Protectionist interests of major Myanmar producers and the military's decision to protect the rice sector as a "key national industry" from foreign investment are stifling productivity at a low level.[52)]

52) German Association for International Cooperation (GIZ), 2015, ibid.

In contrast, liberalization in the production and distribution of legumes has led to a 12-fold increase in production since 1988. Legumes are now the third-highest export earnings in Myanmar after oil and gas. Similar developments would also be possible in rice cultivation and distribution, provided that a modernization of the sector with a foreign chapter is permitted and rigid state regulations and intervention by powerful rice mill operators are prevented. Cambodia has shown through similar reforms that not only can rice production be increased significantly, but also that poverty can be effectively and widely combated.[53)]

Myanmar, the next state of development? Even with the best political will of the new government: the political resistance of the owners and profiteers of the present system will not be within a few years. By sticking to the extractivist growth model, there are few incentives to build a strong, productive industry. Developing countries such as Japan, South Korea and Taiwan have demonstrated that long-term economic transformation is possible through agrarian reform, the establishment of key industries, protectionism-protected export promotion and managed capital markets.[54)]

---

53) German Association for International Cooperation (GIZ), 2015, ibid.
54) German Association for International Cooperation (GIZ), 2015, ibid.

With a long-term development plan, Myanmar could help build and modernize an export-oriented manufacturing industry. Above all in this sector, in the medium term, better paid jobs can be created for hundreds of thousands of workers, which would enable social advancement. So far, the textile sector as the largest manufacturing sector but just twelve to fourteen per-cent of Myanmar's export earnings. While current "low wages" make Myanmar attractive as a potential industrial location, pro-ductivity is too low, given the poor infrastructure and skills of the workers, that the sector will grow without government support.[55)]

While the IMF and the World Bank are pushing for Myanmar's rapid integration into regional and global value chains, without investment in education and training and better capitalization for industry, Myanmar will not be competitive on regional and global markets. The NLD's promised economic transformation and the promised profit sharing of workers can not work without a coherent and state-coordinated industrializa-tion policy. A look to East Asia shows that a »lean state« will hardly be able to tackle this challenge.[56)]

At the end of 2014, Myanmar became a full member of the ASEAN Infrastructure Fund. The three special economic zones

55) German Association for International Cooperation (GIZ), 2015, ibid.
56) German Association for International Cooperation (GIZ), 2015, ibid.

Thilawa, Dawei and Kyaukphyu represent a new industrial and development profile. They also support regional cooperation and integration with the three major economic partners Japan, Thailand and the People's Republic of China. The most advanced Special Economic Zone Thilawa, with its planned area of 2,342 hectares, is seen as a future model for an integrated housing and working concept. Japan holds a 49% stake here and provides funds for the development of basic infrastructure, including electricity, roads, ports and water distribution. The special economic zone Dawei, the supposedly most ambitious industrial zone project of Southeast Asia, is now set to enter its first phase, for which an area of 27 km^2 is planned. Regionally, the economic metropolis of Yangon is one of the focal points of the infrastructure measures.[57)]

The long-term planning for Myanmar's business and business metropolis has been anchored in the »Yangon 2040 Master Plan«. It comprises a total of 80 projects with a total cost of US $ 4.5 billion. This includes a Rapid Bus Transportation System, the Yangon Circular Railway Line and the rehabilitation of the water supply in the Mayangone Township. The dynamically increasing foreign trade necessitates an expansion in the port infrastructure. The port of Yangon Ports is already being ex-

57) Strategiepapier der EG fuer Birma/Myanmar 2007-2013, http://edz.bib.uni-mannheim.de/daten/edz-ma/gdex/07/07_23_de.pdf

panded and will be able to handle 32 container ships simultaneously with the completion of the 14 new berths. In the aviation industry, Yangon International Airport will be modernized by the end of 2015 and designed for a capacity of six million passengers a year.[58)]

The contract for the new major airport Hanthawaddy went to a consortium from Singapore. The airport is geared to doubling the handling capacity. Its completion is scheduled for December 2019. Myanmar aims to more than quintuple its electricity generation capacities from the current 4.4 to 23.6 GW by 2030. The expansion of supply plays an important role in the economic development of the country. So far, only 34.6% of the population have access to the electricity grid. Demand exceeds production by more than a third and is expected to increase by 15% per year. Hydropower currently accounts for 75% of total electricity generation, ahead of natural gas (21%) and coal (4%). The "Electric Master Plan" adopted in 2014 envisages a shift in distribution until 2030, away from hydropower (then only 37%) to more coal (33%) and renewable energies (9%). Renewable energy sources include biomass, geothermal, wind, solar and small hydropower.[59)]

---

58) Strategiepapier der EG fuer Birma/Myanmar 2007-2013, http://edz.bib.uni-mannheim.de/daten/edz-ma/gdex/07/07_23_de.pdf

59) Strategiepapier der EG fuer Birma/Myanmar 2007-2013, http://edz.bib.uni-mannheim.de/daten/edz-ma/gdex/07/07_23_de.pdf

Natural gas should hold its share of the electricity mix at 20%. In order to achieve the goals, enormous investments in power generation and distribution must follow. In particular, the development of renewable energies has presented many challenges to date, including the lack of skilled workers, sources of funding and demonstration objects. So far, foreign players have been involved almost exclusively in expanding the Myanmar electricity supply.[60)]

The World Bank and the Asian Development Bank provide technical support and financial assistance to the government. In general, foreign investment in Myanmar has so far concentrated on the exploration and production of natural gas and crude oil as well as hydropower generation. Foreign companies invested $ 42.8 billion in Myanmar by the end of 2014, of which 38% was already accounted for by the oil and gas sector.[61)]

Second came power generation with 31%. In particular, Chinese companies have expanded hydropower, but in addition to Thailand and India, large-scale western companies from Norway, France, Austria and the United Kingdom are now involved in hydropower projects.[62)]

---

60) Strategiepapier der EG fuer Birma/Myanmar 2007-2013, http://edz.bib.uni-mannheim.de/daten/edz-ma/gdex/07/07_23_de.pdf

61) Strategiepapier der EG fuer Birma/Myanmar 2007-2013, http://edz.bib.uni-mannheim.de/daten/edz-ma/gdex/07/07_23_de.pdf

62) Strategiepapier der EG fuer Birma/Myanmar 2007-2013, http://edz.bib.uni-mannheim.de/daten/edz-ma/gdex/07/07_23_de.pdf

In the future, new fossil-fueled power plants should also satisfy the energy hunger of the country. The largest single project is a lignite-fired power plant, which plans Thailand's largest private power producer Ratchaburi. A smaller natural gas power plant will build the Japanese Sumitomo Corporation in the Special Economic Zone Thilawa. Wind, biomass, geothermal energy and, above all, the sun will form further sources of electricity in the long term. The potential in wind energy is estimated at 365 TWh and in solar energy even at 51,974 TWh per year. The American ACO Investment Group promises to kick-start the use of solar power with two solar farms each with a capacity of 150 MW. Near Dawei, a German company has also installed a small solar farm. Otherwise, the involvement of German companies is still quite low.

2. Innocationsystem

Education

Looking back at education as a core area in the context of the innovation system, one can see the political agenda for 2007-2013. The then government was controlled by the State Peace and Development Council (SPDC). It has reaffirmed its commitment to the achievement of the Millennium Development Goals (MDGs). The government has presented a National Vision Strategy for the period 2001-2010, which aims to build Burma/Myanmar into a modern, developed, self-confident country capable of self-sufficiency and over-provisioning a balanced economy. This should be achieved through appropriate development of the market-based economic system, with the participation of domestic and foreign sources involved with technical know-how and investment in development. From an economic point of view, the main objective is to double GDP within those ten years, which would require an annual growth rate of 5.1%. Reliable data is lacking, and although growth rates are well above the 5.1% threshold, it is unlikely that this will be achieved. Electricity shortages and shortages of imported goods are hindering economic activity and investors are holding back for fear of international sanctions, consumer boycotts and poor overall economic governance.[63]

The then government committed to participate in the Global Education for All initiative, and a National Action Plan has been set up with a framework plan for achieving these goals. Myanmar has set itself the following goals in the context of the EFA initiative[64]:

---

63) Strategiepapier der EG fuer Birma/Myanmar 2007-2013, http://edz.bib.uni-mannheim.de/daten/edz-ma/gdex/07/07_23_de.pdf

64) Strategiepapier der EG fuer Birma/Myanmar 2007-2013, http://edz.bib.uni-mannheim.de/daten/edz-ma/gdex/07/07_23_de.pdf

1) Ensure that significant progress is made by 2015 to enable school-age children to have access to and complete high-quality compulsory and free primary education, 2) Improving all aspects of high quality primary education: teachers, educators and curricula, 3) significant increase in the level of functional literacy and continuing education for all by 2015(4) Safeguarding the learning needs of young people and adults through informal education, teaching basic skills (life skills) and through preventive education programs, 5) developing and improving early childhood education and 6) strengthening education management and EMIS.

The strategies identified in the National Action Plan are implemented only to a very limited extent, as there is a lack of financial resources and trained staff for the administration of the education system. So far, public investment has been used mainly for the construction of new primary schools, while other key areas such as education, textbooks, teachers' salaries and the promotion of pre-primary education have not yet been addressed.[65)]

The education system is chronically underfunded and poorly managed. According to UNICEF, public investment in education

65) Strategiepapier der EG fuer Birma/Myanmar 2007-2013, http://edz.bib.uni-mannheim.de/daten/edz-ma/gdex/07/07_23_de.pdf

declined from 1% of GDP in the 1994/95 school year to 0.3% in the 1999/2000 school year, making it one of the lowest in the world7. One generation at a time is deprived of the opportunity to acquire the skills and capabilities they need to help them tackle their development challenges.[66)]

One of the biggest educational challenges is the low retention and graduation rates, with most departures occurring within the first year (especially in the first three months after starting school).

The number of illiterate and semi-literate students has therefore risen steadily in recent years. In some rural border areas, children from ethnic minority groups have no access to education for a variety of reasons: geographical isolation, internally displaced persons status, poverty or persistent ethnic conflict. When these children attend school, they have difficulty in understanding because they are not powerful in Myanmar. With governments investing so little in education, parents and local communities need to pool their meager resources and provide education services.[67)]

---

66) Strategiepapier der EG fuer Birma/Myanmar 2007-2013, http://edz.bib.uni-mannheim.de/daten/edz-ma/gdex/07/07_23_de.pdf

67) Strategiepapier der EG fuer Birma/Myanmar 2007-2013, http://edz.bib.uni-mannheim.de/daten/edz-ma/gdex/07/07_23_de.pdf

The country was still a long way from achieving access to general primary education despite the official figures. While it is difficult to access specific data, there is still considerable empirical evidence of the extent of the problem. In particular, the administration of the primary education system is poor, the system is significantly underfunded, compounded by wasting resources and poor planning. These serious shortcomings lead to far too low retention rates:

More than half of the children drop out of school before they finish primary school. Socioeconomically, this results in early school leavers who have little or no skills, are particularly at risk, and are at risk of child labor, sexual exploitation, and sexual abuse, as well as trafficking. In areas inhabited by ethnic minority groups, there is also the important challenge of finding generally acceptable ways of dealing with linguistic diversity.

Chapter 6 Innovation System in Laos

I. Country Profile and Historical Characteristics

On the whole, the process of modern country construction in Laos can be roughly divided into the following four stages; 1, May 11th, 1947-November 29, 1957 is the construction period of the constitutional monarchy of the Lao People's Democratic Republic. 2. 1957-December 2, 1986; 3. Dec. 1975-November 1986: Period of highly centralized planned economic system construction; 4. Nov. 1986-present: Construction of Laos modern country with "innovation and opening up" period. The details of each stage are as follows[1) :

First. Lao Constitutional Monarchy (May 1947 - November 1975)

With the victory of the Second World War, Laos has thus ended the centuries-old history of colonial rule and opened a new period of national independence and national construction. The elder sister King Sisavan von signed the decree on May 11, 1947. It is worth mentioning that at this time

1) Vithone Laomao, Administrative Reform of the Lao Government, 2016

Laos issued its first constitution in history. This signifies that Laos, which has just gained national independence, has chosen a constitutional monarchy and has organized state agencies according to the Constitution. The constitution provides that the king has supremacy of power, both as the head of the country and the supreme commander of the army, and as the supreme guardian of Buddhism. The government of the Kingdom of Laos is mainly composed of the prime minister, deputy prime minister, ministers and state secretaries. In 1947, the National Assembly was also established for a four-year term, which was elected by universal suffrage. It is worth mentioning that the king has the right to dissolve the conference.

Second: Before Lao Reform and Opening (November 1947 - November 1975)

In 1957, Laos seized power and established an old people' s democratic republic, which marked the complete victory of the anti-American war and marked a new stage in the administrative reform of Laos. Since then, the Revolutionary Party has become its only ruling party. The Lao Revolutionary Party held the Third Plenary Session of the Second Central Committee. This has historical significance. It made "Laos enter the stage of socialism directly" and the General Assembly pointed out that socialist transformation and socialist construction should be regarded as the most important tasks at present. However, due to the preliminary exploration phase, the Lao Revolutionary Party can be described as "touching the rivers and stones," and it is seriously lacking in the experience of building socialism. It is basically copying the Soviet model and practicing the ultra-left line. In other words, the central government has concentrated on centralization, specifically manifested in the elimination of the capitalist economy and the feudal landlord economy, the active transformation of the individual economy, the establishment and development of the state-owned economy and the collective economy, and the form of agricultural cooperation, and gradually turning scattered and backward small-scale agriculture into For socialist production. In February 1977, Laos held a joint meeting to reaffirm the need to eliminate the capitalist economy and reform the individual economy, reform the relations of production, and establish a socialist nature of production relations in both forms of ownership by the whole people and collective ownership.[2)]

Third, the reform and opening up of the old class (December 19, December 1)

In November 1986, Laos convened the fourth national congress. The meeting put forward the policy of reform and opening up. From then on, it opened the prelude to innovation in Laos. In March 1991, the Fifth National Congress

2) Vithone Laomao, Administrative Reform of the Lao Government, 2016

was convened to confirm that the goal of the Lao People's Revolutionary Party was to lead the people of the country in continuing the reforms and build a prosperous Laos. It proposed the general guidelines for national development and gradually guided Laos into a socialist society.

II. Political Development

Under the influence of socialism system, the Lao Central Government has almost directly taken over all the government affairs, such as the formulation of guidelines and policies, knowledge and behavior, appointment and removal of personnel, procurement of materials, and sales of products. There is no place without any autonomy, let alone autonomy. It just follows the instructions of the Central Government to issue relevant policies, guidelines and orders. During this period, the old description of the relationship between the central government and the local government still has the monarchy. The central leadership is highly centralized and the local government has no rights. The characteristics are specifically expressed in the following aspects: (1) In terms of capital construction, the central ministries of industry manage direct management and arrange the investment and construction tasks of most of the infrastructure projects. Even some of the few local construction projects are mostly directly arranged by the Central Ministry of Industry and the Ministry of Urban Construction, and the local Ministry of Industry does not. (2) In terms of material management, the central government allocates all kinds of important production materials. At the same time, according to the degree of importance, it is allocated by the country or distributed by the heads of central departments. (3) In the aspect of price management, the central government shall lead the main commodity prices uniformly, and the local governments shall manage the prices of secondary commodities at different levels. The provincial, autonomous region, and municipality's management rights are also decentralized by the central government. (4) In terms of financial management, the central unified leadership is adopted to divide revenues and expenditures into different categories. The national finance is mainly divided into the central government, province (special area, municipality directly under the Central Government) and county level 3, but most of the funds are concentrated in the hands of the central government. Central government revenue or expenditure is 100% of total revenue and total expenditure. It can thus be seen that since the establishment of the People's Republic of Qatar, Laos has still implemented a centralized and centralized system during the period of the "one, two and three years" plans. The Lao government has abolished all private-owned enterprises and factories, and prohibited all personal commodity circulation and individual buying and selling businesses, transformed the individual economy, and returned all of them to the state. These factories and enterprises have the nature of state-owned enterprises. In this process, the party's leading organs at all levels have the phenomenon of non-division between the party and the government, such as the party's behalf of the government, and the emergence of the phenomenon of government-to-government enterprises. This has severely constrained the process of administrative reform in Laos.[3)]

III. Economic Transformation and Innovation System

1. Economic Transformation

The Lao People' s Revolutionary Party proposed the policy and mission objectives of "reform and opening up" in accordance with the changes in the political environment at home and abroad and the challenges in reality at the "Big Four" held in November 1986. The Lao party and government will gradually promote the various reforms of the political, economic, social, and cultural systems that are compatible with the socialist objectives of Laos, in order to consolidate and develop Lao' s socialist causes. This marks Laos. Entered a new stage

3) Phouphet Kyophilavong, Evaluation of Macroeconomic Policy in Laos, January 2009, at: https://www.researchgate.net/publication/37504744

of innovation. It is in this context of innovation that the reform of administrative management, which is one of the constituent elements of the upper-level construction, was proposed as an important content of innovation and opening up, which has aroused the attention of party and government departments at all levels.[4)]

At the same time, the prelude to the construction of a modern country in Laos was actually officially delayed until the complete victory of the Laotian people' s struggle against the United States and save the country and the establishment of the Lao People' s Democratic Republic in 1975. This determines that Laos' s reform undertaking has the characteristics of being intertwined with the construction of a modern country, or it can be argued that the "innovation and opening up" business initiated in 1986 was to use innovative ways to promote Laos' modern national construction. Therefore, the reform of the old financial administration has different characteristics from other countries' administrative reforms, namely, "the synchronization of reform and construction". This feature will obviously affect the choice of specific ways and measures for administrative reform in Laos.[5)]

4) Vithone Laomao, Administrative Reform of the Lao Government, 2016
5) Vithone Laomao, 2016, ibid.

In March 1991, the Fifth National Congress was convened to confirm that the goal of the Lao People's Revolutionary Party was to lead the people of the country in continuing the reforms and build a prosperous Laos. It proposed the general guidelines for national development and gradually guided Laos into a socialist society.

Against this background, the Supreme People' s Assembly of Laos adopted the Constitution of the People' s Republic of China on August 14, 1991. This is the first Constitution of the Lao People' s Democratic Republic. This constitution was promulgated and implemented on August 15, the same year. The May 2003 constitutional amendment is the "Lao People's Republic Constitutional Amendment." The Constitution stipulates the national goals of "peace, unity, independence, and democracy" and has initially established the responsibilities of the central and local governments. The Constitution clearly stipulates that the State Council of Laos is the highest state administrative organ. It is delibrated and set up by the National Assembly and is responsible to the National Assembly and the National Assembly. It manages Laos' s political, economic, cultural, resource development, environmental protection, national defense, law and order, and diplomacy. . The specific terms of reference involve social, economic, legal, administrative, and environmental resources. It stipulates that local governments are state administrative organs. Under the authority of the State Council, local governments will administer the kingship, natural resources and people in their jurisdiction, and advance the construction and development of their jurisdiction. (1) It stipulates the status and functions of local governments: Local governments are local level national administrative agencies. They represent the State Council and are responsible to the State Council. They are responsible for managing the political, economic, social, cultural and human resources development and utilization, and natural resources in their jurisdictions. The development and protection of the environment, national security and foreign affairs, and other matters. (2) Clarify the authority of local governments: implement the constitution, laws, resolutions and orders of superiors; formulate areas of strategic planning, social and economic development planning, government budgets, and national prevention and security work plans; , social and cultural, national security and prevention related resolutions, orders and announcements, and the implementation of management; supervision and inspection of the work of various institutions within the jurisdiction; according to the authorization of the State Council to carry out foreign affairs and so on.[6)]

6) Vithone Laomao, 2016, ibid.

At the same time, in clarifying the status and functions of local governments, on November 18, 2011, the Third Central Committee of the Lao PDR passed the draft of "Three Constructions: Provincial Construction as a Local Strategic Unit" and the County as a Comprehensive Self-Strengthening Unit. Hemura is a development unit. It will be implemented on February 15 of the following year. Mainly in the following areas are trial: (1) the development of relevant laws and regulations, implementation plans and related training programs. The Lao government believes that it is a long-term and arduous task to implement the "three constructions" in place. Therefore, the trial should establish an executable and continuous plan, and get scientific, thoughtful, timely guidance and corrections. (2) In terms of working principles, the state should strictly abide by the principle of democratic centralism, and act within the confines of the Constitution and related laws and regulations. (3) Personnel rights, delegating the appointment and dismissal of personnel rights to local governments, such as the powers of the county party committee secretaries and direct directors who have the appointment and dismissal of the director, the provincial party committee secretary and the provincial governor, have the authority to appoint and remove the office level. (4) In terms of economy and finance, the Finance and Taxation Center will give detailed decentralization to local governments at all levels, clearly defining which levels belong to local governments, which are the powers of the central government, and which are the percentages of local governments and the central government. (5) In terms of economic development, local governments at all levels have the right to develop, protect, utilize, and develop economic and cultural resources within their own jurisdiction. However, national defense and diplomatic rights still fall within the jurisdiction of the central government.[7]

Through the above brief review of the process of modern country construction in Laos, it can be clearly demonstrated that for a long time after escaping from colonial rule, due to the influence of international unfavorable factors, the domestic situation in Laos has been difficult to stabilize for a long time, and the country' s construction is also difficult to be normal. The smooth progress of the track, the unrest and the repeated repetition of the state system have caused Laos to miss many favorable opportunities for the development and construction of the country. It was not until the establishment of the Lao People' s Democratic Republic that the long-standing war and turmoil in Laos since its independence was ended, and the state returned to the state of peace building.[8]

7) Vithone Laomao, 2016, ibid.
8) Vithone Laomao, 2016, ibid.

However, at the beginning of the establishment of the new Lao PDR, due to the interference and influence of the "Left" inaccurate ideology, in the aspect of national construction, the Soviet model was fully copied and a highly centralized administration was implemented, which brought a lot of bad to the national construction. The impact caused a certain degree of loss. The "four majors" of the Lao People's Revolutionary Party have made a historical decision to "reform and open up" on the basis of summing up the changes in the political environment at home and abroad and the characteristics of the times, so that the cause of the party and the country has returned to normal development. However, the long-term swinging choice of the political system as the basis of administrative management will inevitably have a profoundly negative impact on the implementation of the Laos' administrative ridge. The most crucial point is that until 1986, Laos opened the door to innovation. In terms of administrative management, Laos has not built up and formed a set of administrative management models to be used as the object of reform. It can be argued that, to a large extent, in terms of administrative management, the composition of construction is greater than that of reform. Together with innovation, it has become a prominent feature of the reform of the old administrative management, which shows that Laos administrative reform will inevitably take on even more arduous tasks and become more urgent.[9)]

2. Innovation system

Education

In the 21st century, education has more and more important to many countries, especially higher education. As a backward country, Laos has also realized the importance of higher education. People who received higher education are not so well educated. Therefore, finding solutions to the difficulties of higher education's development and realizing the popularity of higher education have become the main task that Laos needs to carry out. Laos' s government has regarded developing education as the basic national policy. In 2000, Laos has established an educational reform and has adjusted the legislation of education. In 1962, the Laos government first made education law and adjusted national educational law. However, Laos faces many problems in the process of developing higher education, such as education management, teaching quality, teaching fairness and so on. These problems mainly represent the imperfect educational legislation, the outdated teaching supervision, the imperfect management system, the irregularity of teachers and the outdated teaching equipment. There are the problems in which exist in Laos' higher education by comprehensively analyzes the advantages, the disadvantages, the chance and the

9) Vithone Laomao, 2016, ibid.

challenge of Laos' higher education, such as imitating blindly, lack of theory and practice, lack of system and rules, disorder of higher education development, lack of education subsidy and high-qualified workers, serious profit and rational major plan. In regard to these problems, the author puts forward some related approaches, such as control encrustation rate, raise teaching quality, strengthen system plan, assessment and supervision, add more funds to education, strengthen cultivation of research ability and build predictable system of talents requirements. All these approaches offer suggestions for talents cultivation. The conclusion is that in order to solve these problems, Laos must raise the teaching quality and improve the management of higher education, add more money to education, strengthen the system plan, the assessment and the supervision, and build predictable system of talents requirements et c.[10)]

10) Weiwei, Research on Development Strategy of Higher Education in Lao PDR, 2015

Chapter 7 Conclusion

The phenomenon of progress through innovation has so far been more pronounced in industrialized countries than in developing countries. But even there it is unmistakable that the dissemination and application of modern knowledge and modern technology have become the most important driving force and defining feature in the economy. It is an important task for development policy to support this trend actively and consistently.

This research compares developmental characteristics of the innovation system in the major countries of ASEAN, which are on the transformation.

Vietnam seeks to transform into a knowledge-based economy and society. To this end, the government offers corresponding incentives and invests. In the context of special zones such as business parks, export trade zones, economic zones and high-tech zones, companies are granted further benefits. These zones are spread throughout Vietnam and are being marketed both in Vietnam and abroad to attract further investment.

A paradigm shift in Indonesia was set in the 1990s, when despite legal and political repressions human rights violations denounced and democratic reforms were increasingly demanded. Limited liberalization (keterbukaan), introduced in the late 1980s but withdrawn in 1994, empowered the critical sections of civil society in their struggle for change.

After decades of isolation, Myanmar is now in a phase of social, economic and political change. With the election of ex-General Thein Sein as President in February 2011, far-reaching reforms were launched.

The Lao People' s Revolutionary Party proposed the policy and mission objectives of "reform and opening up" in accordance with the changes in the political environment at home and abroad and the challenges in reality at the "Big Four" held in November 1986.

In this study, education is considered an important element of the innovation system. Education is a key sector for sustainable social and economic development, laying the groundwork for the country's ability to fight poverty and achieve the Millennium Development Goals (MDGs). Education is also a core element of the innovation system. Education is also an important factor in raising environmental awareness and the sustainable use of natural resources indispensable to economic and social development in Southeast Asia.

With the opening of the market in Vietnam, education was also liberalized. In addition to state educational offers, a growing number of private educational institutions is emerging, partly in the form of international cooperation and participation. State responsibilities have been redefined and several comprehensive reforms launched.

After the Indonesian economy has entered a new phase, the Indonesian government stipulates that all public and private college freshmen must take part in the study of Panchakira and only graduate 100 hours before graduating. According to the third long-term development strategy for higher education in 1996, higher education reform must clarify some existing problems.

The government in Myanmar has presented a National Vision Strategy for the period 2001-2010, which aims to build Burma/Myanmar into a modern, developed, self-confident country capable of self-sufficiency and over-provisioning a balanced economy. This should be achieved through appropriate development of the market-based economic system, with the participation of domestic and foreign sources involved with technical know-how and investment in development.

As a backward country, Laos has also realized the importance of higher education. People who received higher education are not so well educated. Therefore, finding solutions to the difficulties of higher education's development and realizing the popularity of higher education have become the main task that Laos needs to carry out.

References

Bettina David, 2012. Machtverschiebungen zwischen Indonesiens Zentrum und Peripherie, in: Aus Politik und Zeitgeschichte, 62 Jahrgang, 11-12.

Boxberger, Gerald 1997. Sozialpolitik und Transformationsprozesse: Kosten der polnischen Transformation und ihre Minderung ueber staatliche Sozialpolitik und Selbsthilfeinitiativen, Frankfurt am Main.

Cooke, Phil., Uranga, M.G., Etxebarria, G. 1997. Regional innovation systems: Institutional and organisational dimensions, Research Policy. 26 (4-5)

Cooke, Phil., Uranga, M.G., Etxebarria, G. 1998. Regional Systems of Innovation: An Evolutionary Perspective, Environment and Planning A, volume 30.

Deutsche Gesellschaft 2016. für Internationale Zusammenarbeit (GIZ) GmbH(ed.) Victnam, Neue Märkte - Neue Chancen, Ein Wegweiser für deutsche Unternehme.

Don K. Marut 2007. Lokale Autonomie: Gemeindeinitiativen für nachhaltigen Frieden, in: Laenderprofil-Indonesien.

Einig, Klaus; Grabher, Gernot; Ibert, Oliver; Strubelt, Wendelin (Hgg.)2005. Urban Governance, in: Informationen zur Raumentwicklung, Heft 9/10.

EKONID(Ed.), Indonesien, Geschäftspotenzial für die energ Nutzung von Geothermie Zielmarktanalyse 2017, www.german-energy-solutions.de.

Eucken, W. 1952. Grundsätze der Wirtschaftspolitik. Bern, Tübingen; Principles of economic policy. Bern, Tübingen.

Feess-D rr, Eberhard 1992. Eine Einfuehrung in die klassische und klassisch-neoricardianische Preis und Verteilungstheorie, Marburg.

Fornahl, Dirk, & Brenner, Thomas 2003. Cooperation, Networks and Institutions in Regional Innovation Systems, Edward Elgar Publishing Ltd.

Freeman, Christopher 1995. The 'National System of Innovation' in historical perspective, Cambridge Journal of Economics. 19(1)

German Association for International Cooperation (GIZ) GmbH (ed.) Vietnam, New Markets - New Opportunities, A Guide for German Companies, 2016

German Trade & Invest (Ed.), 2016. Indonesien, Neue Märkte - Neue Chancen, Ein Wegweiser für deutsche Unternehmer.

Glaeßner, G.J. 1994. Transition und Demokratisierung im Postkommunismus, Opladen

Guocao, The Political System Reform in Vietnam and Its Implications.

Harald Baldersheim, Michal Illner, Hellmut Wollmann 2003. Local Democracy in Post-Communist Europe, Springer.

Henry, John 1990. The Making of Neoclassical Economics, Boston.

iMOVE beim Bundesinstitut für Berufsbildung (BIBB), Marktstudie Vietnam für den Export beruflicher Aus- und Weiterbildung, 2012

Kleinfeld; Plamper; Huber, 2006. Regional Governance, Band 1, Steuerung, Koordination und Kommunikation in regionalen Netzwerken als neue Formen des Regierens.

Kloten, N. 1993. The Time Dimension of the Transition of Economic Systems. In: Wagener HJ. (eds) On the Theory and Policy of Systemic Change. Studies in Contemporary Economics. Physica-Verlag HD.

Kornai, Janos 1992. The Socialist System, Oxford.

Kühne, Olaf 2001. Transformation and Cybernetic System Theory, in: Osteuropa Zeitschrift für Gegenwartsfragen des Osten, Stuttgart.

List, Friedrich 2000. The National System of Political Economy, Kindle Edition

Lundvall, Bengt-Ake 1992. National Systems of Innovation. Towards a Theory of Innovation and Interactive Learning, Pinter Publishers, London.

Marc Frings 2012. Zivilgesellschaft in Indonesien, in: Aus Politik und Zeitgeschichte, 62 Jahrgang, 11-12.

Marinova, Dora, and Phillimore, John. 2003. Models of innovation. In V. Shavinina(Ed.), International handbook on innovation. Amsterdam: Elserver.

Moritz Kleine-Brockhoff 2004. Indonesien: Durchbruch für die Demokratie, Friedrich Ebert Stiftung.

O'Donnell, Guillermo; and Philippe Schmitter 1986. Transitions from Authoritarian Rule: Tentative Conclusions about Uncertain Democracies. Baltimore: Johns Hopkins University Press.

Paraskewopoulos, S. 1991. Erklärungsansätze der Systemtransformation, in: Hartwig, K.-H. und H.-J. Thieme (Hg.), Transformationsprozesse in sozialistischen Wirtschaftssystemen. Ursachen, Konzepte, Instrumente, Berlin, Explanation of the system transformation, in: Hartwig, K.-H. and H.-J. Thieme (ed.), Transformation Processes in Socialist Economic Systems. Causes, concepts, instruments, Berlin.

Pasler, S. Die sozialistische Planwirtschaft der DDR. Konrad-Adenauer-Stiftung e.V., Sankt Augustin/Berlin[The socialist planned economy of the GDR]

Peters, Guy & Jon Pierre 2007. "Governance and Civil Service Systems: From Easy Answers to Hard Questions", p 231-245 in Jos C. N. Raadschelders, Theo A. J. Toonen & Frits van der Meer (eds), The Civil Service in the 21st Century: Comparative Perspectives. Basingstoke: Palgrave.

Phouphet Kyophilavong, Evaluation of Macroeconomic Policy in Laos, January 2009, at: https://www.researchgate.net/publication/37504744

Pierre, Jon (ed) 2000. Debating Governance: Authority, Steering, and Democracy. Oxford: Oxford University Press.

Rothwell Roy 1994. "Towards the fifth-generation innovation process" in International Marketing Review. 11(7): 7-31.

Schueller, A. 1990. Probleme des Uebergangs von der Staatswirtschaft zur Marktwirtschaft, in: Forschungsstelle(ed.).

Stöver, Philip 2012. Demokratisierung und Dezentralisierung, Staatsorganisationsreformen im Kontext von Regime- und Regierungswechseln in Spanien, Polen und Großbritannien.

Thedieck (1999). Governance and Decentralization ", in: Int. Institute of Administrative Sciences, Governance: Concepts and Applications, Brussels

Thedieck (1999). Governance and Decentralisation", in: Int. Institute of Administrative Sciences, Governance: Concepts and Applications, Brüssel

Trippl, M., Maier, G., Tödtling, F., Regional and Urban Economics 2: Regional Development and Regional Policy, Wiesbaden, 2012 (Trippl, M., Maier, G., Tödtling, F., Regional and Urban Economics 2: Regional Development and Regional Policy, Wiesbaden, 2012)

Trippl, M., Maier, G., Tödtling, F., Regional- und Stadtökonomik 2: Regional Entwicklung und Regional Politik, Wiesbaden, 2012 (Trippl, M., Maier, G., Tödtling, F., Regional and Urban Economics 2: Regional Development and Regional Policy, Wiesbaden, 2012)

Vanberg, Viktor 1983. Der individualistische Ansatz zu einer Theorie der Entstehung und Entwicklung von Institutionen, in: Jahrbuch für Neue Politische Ökonomie, hrsg. von Erik Boettcher, Philipp Herder-Dorneich und Karl-Ernst Schenk, Bd. 2, Tübingen.

Vithone Laomao 2016. Administrative Reform of the Lao Government.

Weiwei, Research on Development Strategy of Higher Education in Lao PDR, 2015

Wellesen, Iris 1994. Zur Auslegung des Institutionenbegriffs in der Soziologie.

Wolf, Michael 1998. Transformation als Systemwechsel – eine modelltheoretische Annäherung. In: Hopfmann, Arndt; Wolf, Michael (Hrsg.): Transformation und Interdependenz. Beiträge zu Theorie und Empirie der mittel- und osteuropäischen Systemwechsel (Politische Soziologie, Band 12), Münster.